JUICING
FOR BEGINNERS

1200-DAY OF YUMMY AND EASY RECIPES TO PREPARE HEALTHY AND ENERGIZING JUICES. DETOXIFY YOUR BODY, CLEAR YOUR MIND, AND FEEL VIGOROUS AGAIN

RACHEL SEAN

2023 EDITION

DOWNLOAD YOUR BONUS NOW !

HEART HEALTHY COOKBOOK

E-BOOK

EASY AND TASTY LOW-FAT RECIPES TO KEEP CHOLESTEROL AND BLOOD PRESSURE LEVELS DOWN

i The "Heart Healthy Cookbook" is **100% FREE;** all you need to get is a name and email address. **It's super simple !**

TO DOWNLOAD THE BONUS SCAN THE QR CODE BELOW OR GO TO

https://l.linklyhq.com/l/1g3wP

Scan me

RACHEL SEAN

TABLE OF CONTENT

TABLE OF CONTENT

INTRODUCTION

Introduction

Juicing is basically a process of extracting the liquid content of the raw veggies and fruits. What the process of juicing does is that it segregates and gets rid of the solid matter of the vegetables and fruits which includes the seeds, skin and pulp and retains the liquid juice for consumption. This juice is filled with vitamins, minerals, phyto-nutrients, antioxidants and additional nutrients in its complete natural state.

Juicing Basics

Fruit and vegetable juices are a quick and easy method to include a variety of vitamins and minerals into your diet. All you'll need is some fruit or vegetables, a juicer that separates the pulp from the juice, or a blender for smoothies.

Juices are an easy way to get more vitamins and minerals into your diet because they taste good, especially when you use plenty of ginger for flavor.

But what makes a healthy juice? If you're going to drink your vitamins and minerals, you want to make sure they're balanced out by as many antioxidants as possible. Antioxidants are a substance that stops the oxidation process in the body and prevents cell damage. You can get antioxidants from eating colorful foods—everything from red berries to green leafy vegetables.

Vitamin C is another great antioxidant that you can find in fruits like pineapple and orange to help heal blemishes and prevent infection. Vitamin C also helps combat common colds by repairing tissue damage in the body and boosting your immune system.

Just like you wouldn't drink a glass of chocolate milk to get your multivitamin, it's best to drink juices that contain at least 50% vegetable and fruit juices. Green juices such as kale and celery are full of antioxidants. Juice made from fruits that have a high level of antioxidants, like berries and citrus fruits, also offers a lot of health benefits

Adding some ginger to your juice will help boost its flavor a lot more than if you used nothing but the fruit itself. Ginger doesn't only add flavor, though—it also contains many medicinal properties thanks to its power against nausea, which is why ginger can be helpful for people wanting to ease nausea during chemotherapy or pregnancy.

Juicing Versus Eating Raw Fruits and Vegetables

It's no secret that there are many health benefits to consuming more fruits and vegetables. Unfortunately, it can be difficult to meet your daily quota on a tight schedule! One way you can get your necessary servings is by juicing, but what are the differences between juicing versus eating raw? We've got this information covered for you. Read on to find out which is more convenient, better for a busy lifestyle, has less spoiled food sitting around, has more fiber and nutrients, etc., while also weighing some of the negatives like cost.

Benefits

The inclination or motivation to do something increases when you are aware of all the benefits you stand to gain. Similarly, learning about the different healing benefits of juicing will increase your motivation to add more juices to your daily diet. Here are all the different benefits associated with juicing.

Full-Body Detox

Chlorophyll is a compound in all plants and leafy vegetables that lends them their characteristic green color. Chlorophyll helps the plants absorb sunlight and turn it into energy through a process known as photosynthesis. Your body also obtains a healthy dose of this essential chlorophyll whenever you consume juices.

Why do we need this? It is because chlorophyll is believed to be a natural detoxifying agent. It cleanses the liver and strengthens your body from the inside, eliminates any toxins within, and helps rebuild red blood cells. This green compound helps detoxify your body from the inside. This is also why most detox cleanses, and juices contain leafy vegetables.

One of the primary organs responsible for cleansing and detoxifying your body is the liver. It eliminates the toxins within and purifies your blood too.

Drinking juices made with fresh and wholesome fruit and vegetables daily helps strengthen your liver and promotes your body's detoxification. When there is a build-up of toxins, your energy starts reducing. It also increases the susceptibility to illnesses and diseases. If your liver cleanses itself regularly, then your overall functioning improves too. To attain all these benefits, simply add more juices to your diet.

Anti-Inflammatory Effect

Oxidation is the leading cause of aging and is an internal process that causes the aging of the cells within. Oxidative stress is also a primary risk factor associated with several chronic and severe illnesses and diseases. Whether cardiovascular disorders or poor digestion, oxidative stress is incredibly harmful.

A simple way to counteract oxidation within the body is to increase the consumption of antioxidants. Fresh fruit and vegetables will give your body the required dose of antioxidants. Oxidative stress is also a leading cause of premature aging.

Instead of splurging on beauty and dermatological products, focusing on healthy nutrition will improve your overall sense of being. It also enhances your skin health. When your body is hydrated on the inside, it shows on your skin. Start drinking plenty of juices if you want a healthy glow and supple skin.

Supports Digestion

Your body requires a little energy to digest and assimilate any solid food you consume. However, the energy required to metabolize the juices you drink is much less. This reduces the stress on the digestive system and makes the entire process easier.

You simply need to drink juice, and all the nutrients in it are absorbed by your body without any added energy expenditure.

Boost Immunity

Different fruit and vegetables are rich in a variety of nutrients. For instance, citrus fruits are filled with vitamin C with antioxidant properties.

This essential vitamin is needed for the overall functioning of the immune system and its upkeep. Similarly, some fruit has vitamin B-6, which is needed for improving cognitive functioning.

Several other nutrients are present in different wholesome fruit and vegetables that help tackle inflammation while strengthening the overall function and response of the immune system.

When this system functions effectively and efficiently, it reduces susceptibility to illnesses and ensures any disease-causing pathogens are neutralized before they can cause any damage.

Quick Meal

Vegetable and fruit juices also make for a quick and healthy meal. They hardly take any extra time or effort. You simply need to put the entire components inside a mixer, and voila, the juice is ready. It hardly takes a few minutes to do this. This is incredibly helpful, especially in today's world, where most lead hectic and tiring lives. If you can reduce the time spent in the kitchen, you can redirect it toward something more productive or engage in activities you enjoy. It makes for a quick meal and hardly takes any time to prepare. Also, consuming a nutritious juice hardly takes a few minutes. So, it is not just the cooking time that reduces, but the consumption time also reduces.

For instance, it can take between 10 and 20 minutes to eat a bowl full of salad. After all, you need to slowly chew through all the solid food before swallowing it to ease digestion. On the other hand, how long do you think it takes to drink a glass of carrot juice? You can consume the juice of a bowl full of fruit and vegetables within a few minutes. So, if you are usually in a rush and want to make your life easier, start adding fruit and vegetable juices to your daily diet.

Weight-Loss Potential

Another incredible benefit of adding fruit and vegetable juices to your diet is it promotes weight loss and maintenance. Maybe you want to shed those extra pounds or speed up the process of weight loss, or perhaps you are eager to maintain the weight loss you have already achieved. Whatever it is, juicing is a wonderful idea. You don't have to follow a strict calorie-restricted diet or crash diet to achieve your weight loss and fitness goals. Instead, consume plenty of juices. Your calorie intake automatically reduces when you include healthy and wholesome fruit and vegetable juices while eliminating unhealthy foods. When the calorie consumption is lower than the expenditure, it automatically results in weight loss.

Fill Nutritional Gap

You would have heard at one point or another that you should be eating fresh fruit and vegetables to improve your health. This is because of all the different nutrients they contain. Whether with vitamins and minerals or even digestive fibers, there are plenty of essential nutrients needed for your body's functioning, and vegetables and fruit provide them. Drinking fruit or vegetable juice is a simple yet effective way to fill any nutritional gaps in your daily diet.

Another thing we need to consider is not everyone is comfortable eating a lot of fruit or vegetables. If this applies to you in any way, you need to find a way of adding juices to your diet. If you don't like the idea of eating leafy greens or dislike certain vegetables, why don't you turn them into juice? As mentioned, making juice is easy, and consuming it is easy too. It can take up to 20 minutes to eat 4 carrots but consuming a juice made with 4 carrots takes less than a minute. You can also mix different ingredients to create nutritious combos. You do not have to look any further because this book is filled with a variety of fruit and vegetable recipes that will cater to your body's nutrient requirements. You can do all this without compromising on taste.

Refreshing

Do you usually reach for a cup of coffee or any other caffeinated beverage when you feel a little tired? Do you do this to feel more energetic? Well, did you know that drinking fresh juices would automatically make you feel more refreshed and energetic? It is incredibly easy for the body to absorb nutrients in the juices you drink. All the energy that is not utilized is quickly directed to other processes in your body. Therefore, your energy levels automatically increase. If you are fed up with feeling tired all the time, then start drinking fruit and vegetable juices daily. To feel refreshed, you need not depend on caffeinated beverages or other pre-packaged supplements. Instead, opt for natural substitutes in the form of fruit and vegetable juices.

Promotes Focus

Do you ever feel like you have not had sufficient rest even after sleeping through the night? Do you feel tired in the morning and are fed up with feeling this way? If yes, then the first thing you need to do is concentrate on your diet. What you eat affects your overall energy levels as well as mood. If you take a moment to think about this, it will make perfect sense. How do you feel after eating a large pizza?

On the other hand, how do you feel after eating a bowl of salad or grilled vegetables? The former might make you feel lethargic, while the latter makes you feel lighter and more energetic. Well, here is the answer to your question.

Start drinking more fresh juices if you want to feel refreshed in the morning. All the helpful nutrients in fruit and vegetables also promote cognitive functioning.

They give the brain the required nutrients and energy that improve your ability to stay focused and concentrate.

How To Make Your Own Juices

Even though the process of making juice is as simple as putting fresh fruits and vegetables through your juicer, there are a few things that you should consider doing before you make your first glass of juice. You do not need to worry about peeling or chopping your produce, but you should take the time to wash it first. Even if you purchase organic produce, it could still carry bacteria. Once you've thoroughly washed the produce, you need to prepare your juicer. These preparations will vary depending on the type of juicer. If your juicer has a pulp basket or canister, lining it with a plastic bag will make cleanup easier.

Next, turn the juicer on and feed the produce through it on the speed recommended in the manufacturer's instructions. Keep in mind that it is not always necessary to peel or chop the produce;

nevertheless, you may need to cut it in half or rip huge leaves into smaller pieces in order for it to fit into the feed tubeRefer to the directions provided with your juicer to determine the right speed for different types of produce. (Softer foods like berries may require a low speed while hard produce such as beets or apples will require a higher speed.)

After you finish feeding the produce through the juicer, check the pulp basket or canister. If you find chunks of unprocessed produce, or if the pulp is still wet, feed it through the machine again to extract as much juice as possible.

Once you've finished, you can enjoy your delicious beverage.

It is important to drink your juice as soon as possible after pressing it because, like all fresh foods exposed to air, it could develop bacteria if you let it sit for too long.

If you make more juice than you can consume at one time, supply the extra in a sealed bowl in the fridge for around forty-eight hours. Glass containers are best because plastic may contain BPA (bisphenol A), a chemical that can cause serious health problems. If you do store your juice, fill the container as full as you can manage—over time, excess oxygen in the container may deplete the nutrients in your juice.

Best Fruit And Vegetables For Juicing

The following fruits and vegetables are the most popular choices for juicing. The nutrients and health benefits that have been discovered for each one could fill pages, and research is ongoing. But here are the most notable highlights that you may find interesting and helpful as you explore your juicing options.

a. Fruits

Fresh, raw fruit juice is not only delicious, but it also contains vitamins, minerals, soluble fiber, and important disease-fighting phytonutrients. Inside a meta-analysis of 18 randomized measured trials, feasting of 100 percent fruit juice was not related with an amplified danger of type 2 diabetes and did not negatively affect glycemic control. You can use fruit to sweeten and bring variety to your daily vegetable juice blends and enjoy 100 percent fruit juices on occasion if your health condition allows.

Apple

There is a large variety of apples and choosing from one of them greatly depends on the preference of the juicer; examples include Fuji, Granny Smith, and Golden Delicious. But the main reason you should keep an eye out for apples is that they are packed with antioxidants, dietary fiber, and flavonoids that make them very strong agents against cancer, diabetes, and other severe heart symptoms.

Apricots

Originating from Northern China, apricots are considered to be a very substantial source of vitamin A, potassium, and iron.

Asian Pears

As the name suggests, Asian Pears originate from ancient Asia and are said to be the ancestral version of all the pears that we have familiarized ourselves with today. A single pear holds up to 11% of the level of vitamin C that is generally recommended to be taken every day.

Banana

While bananas are not ideal for fruit juices due to their extremely soft texture, they are still very good sources of vitamins A, B, and C as well as B2, while also adding a fresh flavor to your juice.

Blueberries

Blueberries are the second most popular berry in the United States, and for good reason! These berries are all in all excellent sources of vitamin C and hold a large amount of fiber.

Cherries

Cherries tend to add a delicious sweetness to your juices, while at the same time being a good source of Vitamin C and fiber.

Grapefruit

Originating from the 1800s, seedless grapes and pink seedless grapefruit are known for their exceptionally savory-sweet flavor and richness in vitamin C and fiber.

Lemon

Cultivated in India for the last 2500 years, lemons are known for their smooth and rugged skin texture and abundance of vitamin C.

Lime

While lemons come from India, these little aromatic fruits come from the West Indies and Mexico! These are also abundant in vitamin C, but unlike lemon, these are much less acidic.

Oranges

Fresh oranges are mostly grown alongside the regions of Florida, California, and Arizona. These are annual fruits and can be found all throughout the year.

Oranges are widely known for their high vitamin C contents. Variations include blood oranges, navel oranges, and Valencia oranges.

Tangerine

Tangerines, alternatively called mandarins, are a close relative of oranges. They look similar in texture and boast a sweet flavor with puffy skin. They are rich in vitamins A and C alongside potassium and folate particles.

Cranberries

These are small, round-shaped fruits with a ruby-like color that grow in the marshes and bogs of Northern Europe. These are very rich in vitamin K, C, and A while helping in tackling kidney diseases.

Grapes

These fruits contain a very powerful antioxidant known as polyphenol, which helps in the long run to slow down or even prevent a multitude of cancers such as lung, mouth, and colon cancers.

Kiwifruit

These soft and fleshy fruits originating from Thailand are widely known for their vitamin K and vitamin C contents. But they are also good at supplying other minerals such as copper and a good amount of dietary fiber.

Mango

Cultivated in India, mangoes boast a huge number of benefits ranging from prevention of cancer, decrease in cholesterol levels, improving eyesight, as well as promoting a much healthier sex life.

Melons

Melons contain a good amount of vitamin C and vitamin A in the form of carotenoids as well as potassium, and a range of B complex vitamins that is basically like cherries topped with extra magnesium and fiber contents.

Papaya

Papayas are identified by their smooth and greenish-yellow colored skin. They provide a very delicious flavor that is jam-packed with carotene, flavonoids, vitamin C, pantothenic acid, and various other minerals, including potassium, magnesium, and copper.

Passion Fruit

A fruit that looks like an egg with a pretty thick and hard skin that envelopes a jelly-like golden flesh, these fruits are rich in fiber, the pulp and seeds alone contain 25 grams of fiber! The flesh houses water-soluble antioxidants and vitamin C.

Peaches

Peaches are generally regarded as being treasure troves of minerals that range from iron, manganese, magnesium, zinc, and copper. These are low-calorie fruits with no cholesterol or saturated fat!

Pineapple

A native of Central and Southern America, these discoveries of Christopher Columbus are a rich source of vitamin C! But that's not all; it also encapsulates various other benefits for the human body that includes enhancing the immune system, aiding in digestion, and increasing eye health.

b. *Vegetables*

While many people find it easy to eat fruit, they may not be eating enough vegetables. Fortunately, vegetable juices deliver mind-blowing amounts of nutrition in just a few sips. Juicing dark leafy greens, as well as cruciferous and root vegetables, is without a doubt one of the best ways to ensure a healthy life. I encourage you to make daily vegetable-heavy juices the cornerstone of your healthy eating habits.

Asparagus

The asparagus comes from the Mediterranean area of Southern Europe and has been around for more than 300 years. This is a vegetable from the lily family, and it is jam-packed with a myriad of health benefits! It is a very good source of fiber for starters, and it is also overflowing with vitamins A, E, C, and K, as well traces of important minerals.

Beet

The importance of beet in the world of juicing cannot be stressed enough. Beets are packed with iron, calcium as well as vitamin A. But that's not all, beet juices are extremely effective when it comes to getting rid of the toxins of the body and cleansing the blood.

Broccoli

A vegetable mostly popularized in the US by Italian immigrants, broccolis are good sources of pantothenic acid, dietary fiber, vitamin E, vitamin A, potassium, and a lot of other essential vitamins and minerals.

Brussels Sprouts

These are vegetables hailing from the cruciferous family and are closely related to cabbages and cauliflower. These act as a great source of vitamin B6, potassium, iron, riboflavin, and a host of other goodies.

Cabbage

One of the most ancient leafy plants, cabbage has its roots (literally) planted at the native villages of England and France from where it has now spread in both numbers and popularity. These are mostly famous for their antioxidant related benefits and as an extremely good source of vitamin C.

Carrot

Many of you might not know, but carrots originate from Afghanistan and they have been cultivated in the Mediterranean area since 500 B.C. Carrots are mostly known for their nutritional characteristics that help to protect and improve your eyesight, defend the body against various bacteria, viruses, free radical damage and inflammation and protection against cancer.

Cucumber

Dating back to ancient Babylonian times, cucumbers are often regarded as being the oldest cultivated crop known to mankind. Aside from helping in digestion, cucumbers are very well packed with a complex of B vitamins such as B5, B1, and B7, which help to control anxiety and stress.

Fennel

Fennel is well known for its fiber and folate content, but it is also an essential vegetable for its contribution of phytonutrients and ability to dial down the cholesterol level of blood.

Garlic

Garlic plays a huge role in keeping the body healthy specifically thanks to its impressive attribute of controlling the level of cholesterol in the body by increasing HDL and decreasing LDL levels. This has a direct positive effect on the heart.

While the Greeks disliked it, this was a star among the Europeans.

Ginger

This is a reedy and herbaceous plant that comes in the form of a rootstock and is considered widely to be an Indian produce. Ginger has been used throughout history for its ability to relieve digestive ailments and tackle nausea, motion sickness, and even pain.

Jicama

Often pronounced as hik'-ka-ma, this vegetable is a leguminous one with an extremely large tuberous root. The addition of jicama to your juices will immediately increase the potency of the juice thanks to jicama's unique mixture of vitamins and minerals coupled with phytonutrients and organic compounds such as vitamin C, folate, vitamin B6, manganese, and other essential minerals such as copper.

Kale

This vegetable primarily flourishes during the winter season and is very much known for its similarity to cabbages with the exception of its leaves having much more curls. Kale is often used as both an animal feed as well as human food as it is crowded with vitamin A, C, and good amounts of vitamin B.

Lettuce

This is a vegetable that pre-dates back to 500 B.C. during the Persian age.

Thanks to its sweet and juicy nature, lettuce has been long used as a good ingredient of various kinds of salads and it is an exceptional basis of vitamin A, C, B, and E, with trace amounts of essential minerals of magnesium, iron, and calcium.

Parsley

This is a deviated associate of the carrot family that is believed to have been cultivated during the early years of Sardinia and Italy. Parsley is packed with lots of essential vitamins including C, K, A, and B12. This vegetable helps to strengthen your immune system while fortifying your bones at the same time.

Pepper

Almost a staple product of Mexico, bell peppers were introduced through the escapades of 15th-century Spanish explorers.

Spinach

This vegetable was cultivated long before the Christian era by Greeks and Romans, and highly celebrated by the fictional sailor man **Popeye**! The leaves of spinach are highly concentrated with lots of vitamins such as B, A, C, E, and K alongside phosphorus, iron, and fiber as essential minerals.

String Beans

These are often referred to as Snap Beans and are basically the early pods of kidney beans. They are very good sources of molybdenum! They are also extremely potent sources of folate, copper, and dietary fiber as well as being packed with a generous amount of protein!

Tomatoes

These bubbly, red-colored fruits of Peru are often categorized as being vegetables mainly because of the way they are served to people. These are wells of nutrients and vitamins with substantial amounts of vitamin A, K, C, and a complex of vitamin B6.

Yams and Sweet Potatoes

While these two are different in nature, they are still often mistaken for having the same type of size and texture. These are tall in vitamin C and A and contain decent amounts of fiber and potassium.

Wheatgrass

Wheatgrass comes from the red wheat berry and is a special grass strain that has a very high concentration of vitamins, chlorophyll, vitamins, and activated enzymes amongst other nutrients and minerals. These include phosphorus, magnesium, iron, potassium, the whole vitamin B complex, and vitamin E, C, and K.

Precautions

Though juicing provides many benefits, there are a few precautions you should be aware of before starting a juicing regimen:

• It is more difficult to measure the calories in liquids than in solid foods—if you aren't careful, you can consume a significant number of calories without realizing it.

• If you extend a juice cleanse or fast for more than a few days, your body may become deprived of essential nutrients. As a result, it may slow down your metabolism, which may make weight loss more difficult in the future.

• If you do not transition gradually into a juice cleanse, you may feel deprived and have a difficult time sticking with it.

• Losing weight too quickly on a juicing regimen is unhealthy, and the weight loss you achieve is unlikely to last.

• It is always a good idea to wash your produce before you juice it, and you should also consider going completely organic. Commercial produce is often laced with pesticides and fertilizers that can be damaging to your health.

• The juice you make at home does not contain any preservatives, so its shelf life is much shorter than store-bought juices. As a result, harmful bacteria may creep into the juice if you don't consume it within a day or two.

• If you are fasting while engaging in a juicing regimen, you may experience negative side effects including headaches, dizziness, fatigue, and irritability.

• It is suggested that you check with your doctor before beginning a juicing regimen. Certain individuals, such as those with diabetes, may experience blood-sugar imbalances if they are not careful.

BREAKFAST JUICES

Apple And Lime Juice

Preparation time: 10 mins

Cooking time: 0 mins

Servings: 2

Ingredients:

• 6 large-sized apples, cored and quartered

• 1 tbsp fresh lime juice

Directions:

1. Add apple pieces into a juicer and extract the juice according to the producer's method.

2. Pour into 2 glasses and stir in lime juice.

3. Serve immediately.

Per serving: Calories: 349kcal; Fat: 1.2g; Protein: 1.8g; Carbs: 92.5g

Melony Morning Booster

Preparation time: 8 mins

Cooking time: 0 mins

Servings: 2

Ingredients:

• 2 cups watermelon

• 2 cups cantaloupe

• 2 cups honeydew

• 1/2 lemon

Directions:

1. To prepare the items, you may have to skin, slice, deseed, or mince them.

2. Put a bucket at the spot where the juice will come out of the juicer.

3. Move the components thru the juicer one by one, following the sequence in which they are indicated.

4. After giving this a mix, put the juice into the glasses to serve.

Per serving: Calories: 173kcal; Fat: 1g; Protein: 3g; Carbs: 43g

Juicy Morning Glow

Preparation time: 10 mins

Cooking time: 0 mins

Servings: 3

Ingredients:

• 2 small, sweet potatoes

• 3 carrots

• 3 (organic) apples

• 4 mandarin oranges

• A small piece of fresh ginger

Directions:

1. The sweet potatoes and carrots should both be peeled before being chopped into thin pieces.

2. Apples should be washed, while mandarins and ginger should be peeled.

3. Additionally, slice the fruit into more manageable bits. Extract the juice from every one of the components, then divide it across many glasses and savor.

4. It is possible to keep the juice fresh in the refrigerator for up to two to three days.

Per serving: Calories: 290kcal; Fat: 1g; Protein: 5g; Carbs: 72g

Fresh Sunrise Drink

Preparation time: 10 mins

Cooking time: 0 mins

Servings: 4

Ingredients:

- 1 Pineapple skinned
- 4 carrots washed
- 1 apple, red or green
- 1 lemon juiced distinctly with a citrus juicer
- 1 lime

Directions:

1. Pineapple is prone to clog certain types of juicers; therefore, carrots and apples should be used in alternating fashion. Mix in lemon juice that has been freshly strained.

Per serving: Calories: 174kcal; Fat: 1g; Protein: 2g; Carbs: 45g

Watermelon, Lime, And Ginger Juice

Preparation time: 10 mins

Cooking time: 0 mins

Servings: 2

Ingredients:

- 4 cups seedless watermelon, cubed
- 1 tsp. fresh ginger, skinned
- 1/2 tbsp. fresh lime juice

Directions:

1. Include the entire components to a high-power blender and beat till well combined.

2. Through a cheesecloth-lined sieve, strain the juice and pour it into 2 glasses.

3. Serve immediately.

Per serving: Calories: 95kcal; Fat: 0.5g; Protein: 1.9g; Carbs: 23.5g

Spinach With Basil Refreshing Juice

Preparation time: 10 mins

Cooking time: 0 mins

Servings: 2

Ingredients:

- Handful spinach
- 2 large Swiss chard leaves
- 1 cup of blueberries
- 1/2 lemon
- 8 large basil leaves
- 2 large celery stalks

Directions:

1. To prepare the items, you may be required to skin, slice, de-seed, or mince them.

2. Put a bowl at the spot where the juice will come out of the juicer.

3. Move the components thru the juicer one by one, following the sequence in which they are written.

4. After giving this a mix, put the juice into the glasses to serve.

Per serving: Calories: 118kcal; Fat: 0g; Protein: 1g; Carbs: 30g

Kale With Parsley Morning Drink

Preparation time: 5 mins

Cooking time: 0 mins

Servings: 1

Ingredients:

- 3 pears

- 3 celery sticks
- 4 kale leaves
- Large handful of parsley

Directions:

1. To prepare the items, you may be required to skin, slice, de-seed, or mince them.

2. Put a bowl at the spot where the juice will come out of the juicer.

3. Move the components thru the juicer one by one, following the sequence in which they are written.

4. After giving this a mix, put the juice into the glasses to serve.

Per serving: Calories: 282kcal; Fat: 0g; Protein: 63g; Carbs: 1g

Juicy Morning Blaster

Preparation time: 10 mins

Cooking time: 0 mins

Servings: 2

Ingredients:

- 1 full cucumber
- 2 green apples
- 3 celery stalks
- 2 oranges
- 1/2 lot of spinach

Directions:

1. The entire items should be washed. Cut apples into quarters and scoop out the seeds.

2. Oranges should be peeled, and any seeds should be removed.

3. You can put more spinach leaves inside your juicer if you twist them.

4. Utilizing your juicer, combine every one of the fruits and vegetables.

5. If you so choose, you can either mix this with ice or offer it alongside ice.

6. Mix it up and consume it right away.

Per serving: Calories: 231kcal; Fat: 1g; Protein: 6g; Carbs: 56g

Fresh Morning Juice

Preparation time: 10 mins

Cooking time: 0 mins

Servings: 2

Ingredients:

- 1 cup pineapple, sliced into chunks
- 1 green apple, sectioned
- 1 cup fresh spinach
- 1 leaf kale
- 1 avocado, peeled and pitted

Directions:

1. Press all ingredients through a juicer into a large glass.

2. Stir prior to offering.

Per serving: Calories: 286kcal; Fat: 15g; Protein: 3g; Carbs: 41g

Limey Morning Blast

Preparation time: 10 mins

Cooking time: 0 mins

Servings: 2

Ingredients:

- 1 organic English cucumber with skin on
- 1 handful of spinach
- 1 bunch of organic celery

- 1 lime, skinned
- 1 lemon, skinned
- 1-inch fresh ginger, skinned

Directions:

1. Put single slice of fruit and one bit of vegetable at a moment thru the juicer, utilising a slow juicer or a juice of your choosing, till all of the fruit and vegetables have been squeezed.

2. Relish!

3. To get the most out of juice, drink it right away or preserve it in a bowl made of impermeable glass for almost 24 hours.

Per serving: Calories: 40kcal; Fat: 0.3g; Protein: 1.4g; Carbs: 10g

Early-Berry Juice

Preparation time: 10 mins

Cooking time: 0 mins

Servings: 4

Ingredients:

- 3 large apples
- 3 large pears
- 3 blood oranges
- 2 cups fresh cranberries

Directions:

1. Prep your pears and apples by cutting them down into small enough chunks for your juicer to easily handle.

2. Peel your oranges and cut them into sixths.

3. Add your apples, oranges, and pears to the juicer, then add the cranberries and stir.

4. Store in a bowl for almost seven days, and serve!

Per serving: Calories: 329kcal; Fat: 1g; Protein: 3g; Carbs: 85g

Kale With Beet Red Juice

Preparation time: 5 mins

Cooking time: 0 mins

Servings: 1

Ingredients:

- 2 beets
- 6 carrots
- 2 apples
- 15 kale leaves
- Fresh root ginger, 2-inch (5-cm) piece

Directions:

1. Prepare the materials by peeling, cutting, de-seeding, and/or chopping them as required.

2. Put a bowl at the spot where the juice will come through the juicer.

3. Put each of the components into the juicer separately and in the arrangement that was given to you.

4. After giving it a toss, put the juice into the glasses to serve.

Per serving: Calories: 202kcal; Fat: 0g; Protein: 42g; Carbs: 1g

Juicy Spinach With Apple Lemonade

Preparation time: 5 mins

Cooking time: 0 mins

Servings: 1

Ingredients:

- 2 apples
- 4 handfuls of spinach

- 16 kale leaves
- 1 cucumber
- 4 celery sticks
- 2 lemons

Directions:

1. To prepare the items, you may be required to skin, slice, de-seed, or mince them.

2. Put a bowl at the spot where the juice will come out of the juicer.

3. Move the components thru the juicer one by one, following the sequence in which they are written.

4. After giving this a mix, put the juice into the glasses to serve.

Per serving: Calories: 176kcal; Fat: 0g; Protein: 35g; Carbs: 1g

Strawberry And Parsley Juice

Preparation time: 10 mins

Cooking time: 0 mins

Servings: 2

Ingredients:

- 2 1/2 cups fresh ripe strawberries, hulled
- 2 tbsp fresh parsley
- 1 cup of filtered water
- 1 tsp fresh lime juice
- Tweak of salt

Directions:

1. Add the entire components to a high-power mixer and beat them until well combined.

2. Through a cheesecloth-lined sieve, strain the juice and pour it into 2 glasses.

3. Serve immediately.

Per serving: Calories: 59kcal; Fat: 0.6g; Protein: 1.3g; Carbs: 14.1g

Peach And Apple Morning Delight

Preparation time: 5 mins

Cooking time: 0 mins

Servings: 1

Ingredients:

- 1 sweet potato
- 2 ripe peaches (or use pears)
- 1 apple
- 1 1/3 cups (150 g/6 oz) blueberries
- Dash of ground icinnamon

Directions:

1. To prepare the items, you may be required to skin, slice, de-seed, or mince them.

2. Put a bowl at the spot where the juice will come out of the juicer.

3. Move the components thru the juicer one by one, following the sequence in which they are written.

4. After giving this a mix, put the juice into the glasses to serve.

Per serving: Calories: 352kcal; Fat: 0g; Protein: 83g; Carbs: 1g

Morning Cucumber And Berry Chard

Preparation time: 5 mins

Cooking time: 0 mins

Servings: 2

Ingredients:

- 1 cup pineapple

- 1 cup of raspberries
- 2 large celery stalks
- 2 Swiss chard leaves
- 1/2 cucumber

Directions:

1. To prepare the items, you may be required to skin, slice, de-seed, or mince them.

2. Put a bowl at the spot where the juice will come out of the juicer.

3. Move the components thru the juicer one by one, following the sequence in which they are written.

4. After giving this a mix, put the juice into the glasses to serve.

Per serving: Calories: 200kcal; Fat: 0g; Protein: 2g; Carbs: 51g

Gingered Chard Red Juice

Preparation time: 5 mins

Cooking time: 0 mins

Servings: 1

Ingredients:

- 2 beets
- 4 carrots
- 4 oranges
- 8 chard leaves
- Fresh root ginger, 2-inch (5-cm) piece (optional)

Directions:

1. To prepare the items, you may be required to skin, slice, de-seed, or mince them.

2. Put a bowl at the spot where the juice will come out of the juicer.

3. Move the components thru the juicer one by one, following the sequence in which they are written.

4. After giving this a mix, put the juice into the glasses to serve.

Per serving: Calories: 159kcal; Fat: 0g; Protein: 34g; Carbs: 1g

Green Citrus Drink

Preparation time: 5 mins

Cooking time: 0 mins

Servings: 1

Ingredients:

- 4 apples
- 4 oranges
- 12 handfuls iof ileafy igreens i(e.g., ikale, ichard, spinach, ior romaine lettuce)

Directions:

1. To prepare the items, you may be required to skin, slice, de-seed, or mince them.

2. Put a bowl at the spot where the juice will come out of the juicer.

3. Move the components thru the juicer one by one, following the sequence in which they are written.

4. After giving this a mix, put the juice into the glasses to serve.

Per serving: Calories: 216kcal; Fat: 0g; Protein: 49g; Carbs: 1g

Passionfruit Juice

Preparation time: 10 mins

Cooking time: 0 mins

Servings: 2

Ingredients:

- 1/2 cup passion fruit pulp
- 2 tbsps. sugar
- 2 tsp. fresh lemon juice
- 2 cups filtered water

Directions:

1. Include the entire components to a high-power mixer and pulse till well combined.

2. Through a cheesecloth-lined sieve, strain the juice and pour it into 2 glasses.

3. Serve immediately.

Per serving: Calories: 103kcal; Fat: 0.5g; Protein: 1.3g; Carbs: 25.9g

Pineapple And Orange Juice

Preparation time: 10 mins

Cooking time: 0 mins

Servings: 2

Ingredients:

- 2 cups fresh pineapple, chopped
- 4 oranges, skinned, seeded, and sectioned
- 2 tsps. sugar
- Tweak of salt and ground black pepper
- 1 cup of filtered water

Directions:

1. Include the entire components to a high-power blender and pulse till well combined.

2. Through a cheesecloth-lined sieve, strain the juice and pour it into 2 glasses.

3. Serve immediately.

Per serving: Calories: 270kcal; Fat: 0.6g; Protein: 4.4g; Carbs: 68.9g

FRUIT-BASED JUICES

Beet With Berry And Apple Juice

Preparation time: 5 mins

Cooking time: 0 mins

Servings: 2

Ingredients:

- 2 cups blueberries
- 2 small beets
- 1 small apple

Directions:

1. To prepare the items, you may be required to skin, slice, de-seed, or mince them.

2. Put a bowl at the spot where the juice will come out of the juicer.

3. Move the components thru the juicer one by one, following the sequence in which they are written.

4. After giving this a mix, put the juice into the glasses to serve.

Per serving: Calories: 317kcal; Fat: 2g; Protein: 5g; Carbs: 79g

Pomegranate Juice

Preparation time: 10 minutes

Cooking time: 0 minutes

Servings: 2

Ingredients:

- 5 large-sized pomegranates, arils removed

Directions:

1. Add the pomegranates arils to a high-power blender and pulse for about 15–20 seconds.

2. Through a cheesecloth-lined sieve, strain the juice by pressing the seeds with a back of a spoon.

3. Pour the juice into four glasses and serve immediately.

Per serving: Calories: 250kcal; Fat: 0g; Protein: 2.5g; Carbs: 65g

Grapefruit Juice With Lemon And Orange

Preparation time: 5 minutes

Cooking time: 1 minute

Servings: 1–2

Ingredients:

- 3 navel oranges
- 3 grapefruits
- 2 lemons

Directions:

1. Prepare all ingredients—cut, wash, peel, and deseed, when possible.

2. Put them into a juicer and process until smooth.

3. Add enough water and sugar to get the desired sweetness and consistency (optional).

4. Pour into a glass (optionally through a sieve).

5. Enjoy!

Per serving: Calories: 100kcal; Fat: 1g; Protein: 1g; Carbs: 34g

Cherry Juice

Preparation time: 10 minutes

Cooking time: 0 minutes

Servings: 2

Ingredients:

• 4 cups fresh cherries, pitted

• 1/2 cup filtered water

Directions:

1. Add cherries and water to a high-power blender and pulse until well combined.

2. Through a cheesecloth-lined sieve, strain the juice and pour it into 3 glasses.

3. Serve immediately.

Per serving: Calories: 180kcal; Fat: 0g; Protein: 4g; Carbs: 44g

Juicy Tropical Island

Preparation time: 10 minutes

Cooking time: 0 minutes

Servings: 1

Ingredients:

• 1 large apple

• 1 large orange (peeled)

• 1 pinch cayenne pepper (spice)

• 1 mango (peeled)

• 1/2 lemon (peeled)

Directions:

1. Wash the fruits and vegetables thoroughly

2. Put them through the juicer and enjoy

Per serving: Calories: 245kcal; Fat: 1g; Protein: 4g; Carbs: 73g

Plum Juice

Preparation time: 10 minutes

Cooking time: 0 minutes

Servings: 4

Ingredients:

• 4 cups ripe plums, pitted and chopped

• 2 tbsp maple syrup

• 1 cup of filtered water

Directions:

1. Add all ingredients to a high-power blender and pulse until well combined.

2. Through a cheesecloth-lined sieve, strain the juice and pour it into 4 glasses.

3. Serve immediately.

Per serving: Calories: 112kcal; Fat: 0.4g; Protein: 1g; Carbs: 29.4g

Apple And Grapes Juice

Preparation time: 10 minutes

Cooking time: 0 minutes

Servings: 2

Ingredients:

• 5 large-sized green apples, cored and quartered

• 2 cups seedless grapes

• 2 tsp fresh lime juice

Directions:

1. Add all ingredients into a juicer and extract the juice according to the manufacturer's method.

2. Pour into 2 glasses and serve immediately.

Per serving: Calories: 352kcal; Fat: 1.3g; Protein: 2.1g; Carbs: 92.8g

Sugared Avocado With Lemon Water

Preparation time: 5 minutes

Cooking time: 0 minutes

Servings: 2

Ingredients:

- 1 avocado, halved
- 4 cups (950 ml/32 fl oz) water
- 1/2 cup (120 ml/4 fl oz) lemon juice or lime juice
- 1/2 cup (100 g) sugar, plus more to taste

Directions:

1. Scoop the avocado into a blender. Add the rest of the ingredients and blend until smooth.

2. Add more sugar to taste, if desired. Serve over ice.

Per serving: Calories: 271kcal; Fat: 15g; Protein: 2g; Carbs: 38g

Berry With Sparkling Pomegranate Juice

Preparation time: 5 minutes

Cooking time: 0 minutes

Servings: 2

Ingredients:

- 2 cups raspberries
- 2 ripe pomegranates
- 1 cup sparkling water

Directions:

1. Peel and remove the seeds from the pomegranate.

2. Place a container under the juicer's spout.

3. Feed the raspberries and pomegranate seeds through the juicer.

4. Stir the sparkling water into the juice and pour into glasses to serve.

Per serving: Calories: 467kcal; Fat: 4g; Protein: 6g; Carbs: 113g

Homemade Avocado Juice

Preparation time: 5 minutes

Cooking time: 0 minutes

Servings: 1

Ingredients:

- 1 medium avocado, pitted and peeled
- 3 medium peaches, pitted and peeled
- 1/4 cup Greek yogurt

Directions:

1. Slice up the peaches and avocado and throw them in the blender.

2. Add the yogurt to the blender.

3. Process together the three ingredients in a blender.

4. This incredible combination is not only delicious but provides many essential nutrients. The avocado is jam-packed with essential oils and fats. Despite popular belief, these healthy fats are an important key to fat loss.

Per serving: Calories: 522kcal; Fat: 30g; Protein: 12g; Carbs: 62g

Banana Blackberry Fruit Juice

Preparation time: 5 minutes

Cooking time: 0 minutes

Servings: 2

Ingredients:

- 2 cups blackberries
- 1 medium apple
- 1 small banana

Directions:

1. Peel, cut, deseed, and/or chop the ingredients as needed.

2. Place a container under the juicer's spout.

3. Feed the blackberries and apples through the juicer.

4. In a blender, blend the banana until smooth.

5. Stir the pureed banana into the juice and pour it into glasses to serve.

Per serving: Calories: 328kcal; Fat: 1g; Protein: 4g; Carbs: 83g

Blueberry And Pineapple Juice

Preparation time: 10 minutes

Cooking time: 0 minutes

Servings: 2

Ingredients:

- 2–3 cups fresh pineapple chunks
- 2 cups fresh blueberries
- 1 (1/2-inch) piece of fresh ginger, peeled

Directions:

1. Add all ingredients into a juicer and extract the juice according to the manufacturer's method.

2. Pour into 2 glasses and serve immediately.

Per serving: Calories: 174kcal; Fat: 0.9g; Protein: 2.2g; Carbs: 44.6g

Berry With Cilantro And Banana Juice

Preparation time: 5 minutes

Cooking time: 0 minutes

Servings: 2

Ingredients:

- 2 cups strawberries
- 1 cup cilantro
- 1 cup of cold water
- 1 small banana

Directions:

1. Peel, cut, deseed, and/or chop the ingredients as needed.

2. Place a container under the juicer's spout.

3. Feed the strawberries and cilantro through the juicer.

4. In a blender, combine the water and banana and blend until smooth.

5. Add the strawberry cilantro juice and pulse to blend.

6. Pour into glasses and serve.

Per serving: Calories: 92kcal; Fat: 1g; Protein: 2g; Carbs: 23g

Grapy Berry With Apple Juice

Preparation time: 5 minutes

Cooking time: 0 minutes

Servings: 2

Ingredients:

- 1 ripe grapefruit
- 1 cup of blueberries
- 1 cup of red grapes

- 1 small apple

Directions:

1. Peel, cut, deseed, and/or chop the ingredients as needed.

2. Place a container under the juicer's spout.

3. Feed the ingredients one at a time, in the order listed, through the juicer.

4. Stir the juice and pour it into glasses to serve.

Per serving: Calories: 489kcal; Fat: 2g; Protein: 5g; Carbs: 125g

Watermelon, Plum, And Cherry Juice

Preparation time: 10 minutes

Cooking time: 0 minutes

Servings: 2

Ingredients:

- 2 1/2 cups seedless watermelon, cut into chunks
- 3 plums, pitted and halved
- 15 fresh red cherries
- 4 ice cubes

Directions:

1. Add all ingredients to a high-power blender and pulse until well combined.

2. Through a cheesecloth-lined sieve, strain the juice and pour it into 2 glasses.

3. Serve immediately.

Per serving: Calories: 141kcal; Fat: 0.6g; Protein: 2.8g; Carbs: 35.9g

Orange, Carrot, And Lemon Juice

Preparation time: 5 minutes

Cooking time: 1 minute

Servings: 1–2

Ingredients:

- 5 oranges
- 3 medium carrots
- 1 lemon
- 1 small piece of ginger
- 1 tbsp ground turmeric
- 1–2 tbsp honey (optional)

Directions:

1. Prepare all ingredients—cut, wash, peel, and deseed, when possible.

2. Put them into a juicer and process until smooth.

3. Add enough water and sugar to get the desired sweetness and consistency (optional).

4. Pour into a glass (optionally through a sieve).

5. Stir in turmeric and honey.

6. Enjoy!

Per serving: Calories: 110kcal; Fat: 1g; Protein: 3g; Carbs: 40g

Grape Nectar Juice

Preparation time: 5 minutes

Cooking time: 5 minutes

Servings: 1–2

Ingredients:

- 6 lychees
- 6 lemon chunks
- 2 tbsp sugar syrup
- 1/8 cup crushed ice per serving
- 1/2 cup black grape juice per serving

Directions:

1. Prepare all ingredients—cut, wash, peel, and deseed, when possible.

2. Put them into a juicer and process until smooth.

3. Add enough water and sugar to get the desired sweetness and consistency (optional).

4. Pour into a glass (optionally through a sieve), add grape juice and crushed ice.

5. Enjoy!

Per serving: Calories: 100kcal; Fat: 1g; Protein: 6g; Carbs: 49g

Orange Basil Juice

Preparation time: 5 minutes

Cooking time: 1 minute

Servings: 1–2

Ingredients:

- 2 oranges
- 6 basil leaves
- Drizzle of honey, optional
- 4–5 ice cubes

Directions:

1. Prepare all ingredients—cut, wash, peel, and deseed, when possible.

2. Put them into a juicer and process until smooth.

3. Add enough water and sugar to get the desired sweetness and consistency (optional).

4. Pour into a glass filled with the ice cubes (optionally through a sieve), and garnish with a few basil leaves.

5. Enjoy!

Per serving: Calories: 116kcal; Fat: 1g; Protein: 2g; Carbs: 46g

Orange Juice

Preparation time: 10 minutes

Cooking time: 0 minutes

Servings: 2

Ingredients:

- 6 large-sized oranges, peeled, seeded and sectioned

Directions:

1. Add orange pieces into a juicer and extract the juice according to the manufacturer's method.

2. Pour into 2 glasses and serve immediately.

Per serving: Calories: 259kcal; Fat: 0.7g; Protein: 5.2g; Carbs: 64.9g

Cilantro Kiwi Juice Blend

Preparation time: 5 minutes

Cooking time: 0 minutes

Servings: 2

Ingredients:

- 2 cups blackberries
- 2 ripe kiwis
- 1 medium apple
- 6 sprigs of cilantro

Directions:

1. Peel, cut, deseed, and/or chop the ingredients as needed.

2. Place a container under the juicer's spout.

3. Feed the ingredients one at a time, in the order listed, through the juicer.

4. Stir the juice and pour it into glasses to serve.

Per serving: Calories: 284kcal; Fat: 1g; Protein: 3g; Carbs: 72g

VEGETABLE-BASED JUICES

Citrus Apple, Spinach, And Celery Juice

Preparation time: 10 minutes

Cooking time: 0 minutes

Servings: 2

Ingredients:

- 3 cups fresh spinach, chopped
- 4 large-sized celery stalks, chopped
- 2 large-sized green apples, cored and quartered
- 1 large-sized orange, peeled, seeded, and sectioned
- 1 tbsp fresh lime juice
- 1 tbsp fresh lemon juice

Directions:

1. Add all ingredients into a juicer and extract the juice according to the manufacturer's method.

2. Pour into 2 glasses and serve immediately.

Per serving: Calories: 178kcal; Fat: 0.8g; Protein: 3g; Carbs: 44.5g

Arugula Watermelon Juice

Preparation time: 5 minutes

Cooking time: 1 minute

Servings: 1–2

Ingredients:

- 1 handful arugula
- 1/4 slice watermelon
- 1/2 lime
- 2 celery stalks

Directions:

1. Prepare all ingredients—cut, wash, peel and deseed, when possible.

2. Put them into a juicer and process until smooth.

3. Add enough water and sugar to get the desired sweetness and consistency (optional).

4. Pour into a glass (optionally through a sieve), serve chilled.

5. Enjoy!

Per serving: Calories: 80kcal; Fat: 1g; Protein: 1g; Carbs: 29g

Horseradish Beet Juice

Preparation time: 5 minutes

Cooking time: 1 minute

Servings: 1–2

Ingredients:

- 1 small red beet
- 1 celery rib
- 1 lb apple
- 1 1/4 to 1 1/2 oz piece of horseradish
- 1/2 tbsp rosemary leaves
- 1 tbsp lemon juice
- A pinch of salt

Directions:

1. Prepare all ingredients— cut, wash, peel and deseed, when possible.

2. Put them into a juicer and process until smooth.

3. Add water to get the desired thickness (optional).

4. Pour into a glass (optionally through a sieve).

5. Stir in the lemon juice and a pinch of salt, and serve chilled.

6. Enjoy!

Per serving: Calories: 119kcal; Fat: 1g; Protein: 1g; Carbs: 35g

Kiwi Grape Green Juice

Preparation time: 5 minutes

Cooking time: 5 minutes

Servings: 1 - 2

Ingredients:

- 2 1/2 field cucumbers
- 1 cup green grapes
- 1/2 cup spinach
- 2 small kiwis
- 1–2 cups of water

Directions:

1. Prepare all ingredients—cut, wash, peel and deseed, when possible.

2. Put them into a juicer and process until smooth.

3. Add enough water and sugar to get the desired sweetness and consistency (optional).

4. Pour into a glass (optionally through a sieve), serve chilled.

5. Enjoy!

Per serving: Calories: 106kcal; Fat: 1g; Protein: 2g; Carbs: 39g

Pear, Spinach, Celery, And Parsley Juice

Preparation time: 10 minutes

Cooking time: 0 minutes

Servings: 2

Ingredients:

- 3 cups fresh spinach
- 6 large-sized celery stalks
- 2 medium-sized pears, cut into eighths
- 1/2 cup fresh parsley
- 1/2 lemon, peeled

Directions:

1. Add all ingredients into a juicer and extract the juice according to the manufacturer's method.

2. Pour into 2 glasses and serve immediately.

Per serving: Calories: 146kcal; Fat: 0.7g; Protein: 2.9g; Carbs: 36.3g

Broccoli With Mellow Celery

Preparation time: 5 minutes

Cooking time: 0 minutes

Servings: 1

Ingredients:

- 4 celery ribs
- 1 cucumber
- 2 cups broccoli
- 1/2 lemon

Directions:

1. Wash all the ingredients.

2. Trim the ends from the celery and cucumber, then cut into 4-inch pieces.

3. Remove the stalk from the broccoli crown with a knife and discard or save it to juice later. Cut the crown into small florets.

4. Peel the lemon and cut it into quarters.

5. Place a pitcher under the juicer's spout to collect the juice.

6. Feed each ingredient through the juicer's intake tube in the order listed.

7. When the juice stops flowing, remove the pitcher and stir the juice.

8. Serve immediately.

Per serving: Calories: 148kcal; Fat: 2g; Protein: 14g; Carbs: 41g

Parsley With Lettuce Special

Preparation time: 5 minutes

Cooking time: 0 minutes

Servings: 1

Ingredients:

- 2 cups romaine lettuce (about 4 leaves)
- 2 tbsp parsley leaves
- 1/2 green apple
- 1/2 beet
- 1 lemon

Directions:

1. Wash all the ingredients.

2. Remove the apple core and discard. Cut the apple into quarters, leaving the peel intact.

3. Remove any greens from the beet and save them for juicing later. Cut the beet into quarters.

4. Peel the lemon and cut it into quarters.

5. Place a pitcher under the juicer's spout to collect the juice.

6. Feed each ingredient through the juicer's intake tube in the order listed.

7. When the juice stops flowing, remove the pitcher and stir the juice.

8. Serve immediately.

Per serving: Calories: 63kcal; Fat: 1g; Protein: 3g; Carbs: 21g

Spinach Vegetable Juice

Preparation time: 5 minutes

Cooking time: 1 minute

Servings: 1–2

Ingredients:

- 5 small stalks of celery
- 4-inch piece ginger
- 3 small green apples
- 1 cup spinach
- 1/2 medium lemon
- 1/2 cup parsley
- 1 cup romaine

Directions:

1. Prepare all ingredients—cut, wash, peel and deseed, when possible.

2. Put them into a juicer and process until smooth.

3. Add enough water and sugar to get the desired sweetness and consistency (optional).

4. Pour into a glass (optionally through a sieve), serve chilled.

5. Enjoy!

Per serving: Calories: 94kcal; Fat: 3g; Protein: 2g; Carbs: 38g

Tomato Beet Multi Juice

Preparation time: 5 minutes

Cooking time: 1 minute

Servings: 1–2

Ingredients:

- 1 small beet
- 1 large tomato
- 1 small red pepper
- 1 small fennel bulb
- 1 cucumber
- 3 celery stalks
- 2 large carrots
- 1 handful parsley
- 1 lemon

Directions:

1. Prepare all ingredients—cut, wash, peel and deseed, when possible.

2. Put them into a juicer and process until smooth.

3. Add enough water and sugar to get the desired sweetness and consistency (optional).

4. Pour into a glass (optionally through a sieve), serve chilled.

5. Enjoy!

Per serving: Calories: 118kcal; Fat: 1g; Protein: 5g; Carbs: 31g

Gingered Carrot With Oregano Green Juice

Preparation time: 5 mins

Cooking time: 0 mins

Servings: 1

Ingredients:

- 1 to 2 stalks of celery
- 1 green apple, seeds detached
- 1 large orange, skinned
- 1 small bunch of organic kale
- 2 small handfuls of spinach
- 1-inch piece of fresh ginger
- 1 big icarrot
- Freshly squeezed lemon juice, as required
- 2 to 3 ice cubes

Directions:

1. Thoroughly wash the fruits and vegetables.

2. Run through a juicer and pour into a tall glass.

3. Stir in the freshly squeezed lemon juice to your taste, add 2 to 3 ice cubes and enjoy.

Per serving: Calories: 251kcal; Fat: 9g; Protein: 8g; Carbs: 36g

Carrot Celery And Cucumber Juice

Preparation time: 5 mins

Cooking time: 1 min

Servings: 1–2

Ingredients:

- 5 carrots
- 1 small cucumber
- 4 celery stalks
- 1 apple
- 1 beet
- 1/2 lemon

Directions:

1. Prepare all ingredients—cut, wash, peel and deseed, when possible.

2. Put them into a juicer and process until smooth.

3. Add enough water and sugar to get the desired sweetness and consistency (optional).

4. Pour into a glass (optionally through a sieve), serve chilled.

5. Enjoy!

Per serving: Calories: 112kcal; Fat: 1g; Protein: 3g; Carbs: 39g

Cucumber Grape Juice

Preparation time: 5 mins

Cooking time: 1 min

Servings: 1–2

Ingredients:

- 1/2 of cucumber
- 2 cups green grapes
- 1 green apple
- 6 chard leaves
- 1-inch piece of ginger

Directions:

1. Prepare all ingredients—cut, wash, peel and deseed, when possible.

2. Put them into a juicer and process until smooth.

3. Add enough water and sugar to get the desired sweetness and consistency (optional).

4. Pour into a glass (optionally through a sieve), serve chilled.

5. Enjoy!

Per serving: Calories: 72kcal; Fat: 1g; Protein: 3g; Carbs: 27g

Cucumber Carrot Juice

Preparation time: 5 mins

Cooking time: 1 min

Servings: 1–2

Ingredients:

- 6 strawberries
- 1 big cucumber
- 1 big red apple
- 2 average carrots

Directions:

1. Prepare all ingredients—cut, wash, peel and deseed, when possible.

2. Put them into a juicer and process until smooth.

3. Add enough water and sugar to get the desired sweetness and consistency (optional).

4. Pour into a glass (optionally through a sieve), serve chilled.

5. Enjoy!

Per serving: Calories: 79kcal; Fat: 0g; Protein: 1g; Carbs: 34g

Watermelon With Kale Green Juice

Preparation time: 5 mins

Cooking time: 0 mins

Servings: 1

Ingredients:

- 1 1/2 cups watermelon
- 4 kale leaves
- 1/2 lime
- 2 celery ribs

Directions:

1. Wash the kale, lime, and celery.

2. Cut the watermelon into quarters. Remove the rind and discard. Cut the watermelon into smaller pieces.

3. Slender the ends from the celery, afterwards slice into 4-inch pieces.

4. Peel the lime in half and cut it into quarters.

5. Put a pitcher below the juicer's spout to collect the juice.

6. Feed each ingredient through the juicer's intake tube in the order listed.

7. When the juice stops flowing, remove the pitcher and stir the juice.

8. Serve instantly.

Per serving: Calories: 90kcal; Fat: 1g; Protein: 6g; Carbs: 24g

Fat Burner Juice

Preparation time: 5 mins

Cooking time: 1 min

Servings: 1–2

Ingredients:

• 1 bunch of dandelion greens

• 1/2 head of green cabbage

• 1/2 bunch celery

• 1 or 2 inches of ginger root

• 1/2 lemon

Directions:

1. Prepare all ingredients—cut, wash, peel and deseed, when possible.

2. Put them into a juicer and process until smooth.

3. Add enough water and sugar to get the desired sweetness and consistency (optional).

4. Pour into a glass (optionally through a sieve), serve chilled.

5. Enjoy!

Per serving: Calories: 71kcal; Fat: 1g; Protein: 4g; Carbs: 29g

Detox Celery Juice

Preparation time: 5 mins

Cooking time: 1 min

Servings: 1–2

Ingredients:

• 15 oz. celery

Directions:

1. Juice until smooth.

2. Add enough water and sugar to get the desired sweetness and consistency (optional).

3. Pour into a glass (optionally through a sieve), serve chilled.

4. Enjoy!

Per serving: Calories: 84kcal; Fat: 2g; Protein: 4g; Carbs: 39g

Purple Haze Juice

Preparation time: 5 mins

Cooking time: 1 min

Servings: 1–2

Ingredients:

• 1 medium beet

• 1 large Granny Smith apple

• 1 medium carrot

• 1 medium orange

- 1 4-inch piece of ginger
- 1/8 tsp fine Himalayan pink salt

Directions:

1. Prepare all ingredients—cut, wash, peel and deseed, when possible.

2. Put them into a juicer and process until smooth.

3. Add enough water and sugar to get the desired sweetness and consistency (optional).

4. Pour into a glass (optionally through a sieve), serve chilled.

5. Enjoy!

Per serving: Calories: 82kcal; Fat: 1g; Protein: 4g; Carbs: 31g

Radish Beet Juice

Preparation time: 5 mins

Cooking time: 1 min

Servings: 1–2

Ingredients:

- 1 radish
- 1 small red beet
- 2 handfuls of watercress
- 18 baby carrots
- 1 handful of baby spinach
- 1 gala apple
- 2 tbsps. honey

Directions:

1. Prepare all ingredients—cut, wash, peel and deseed, when possible.

2. Put them into a juicer and process until smooth.

3. Add enough water and sugar to get the desired sweetness and consistency (optional).

4. Pour into a glass (optionally through a sieve).

5. Add honey, serve chilled.

6. Enjoy!

Per serving: Calories: 129kcal; Fat: 1g; Protein: 3g; Carbs: 38g

Lemony Kale And Celery Green Juice

Preparation time: 5 mins

Cooking time: 0 mins

Servings: 2

Ingredients:

- 2 green apples, halved
- 4 stalks of celery
- 1 cucumber, peeled
- 6 romaine leaves
- 5 kale leaves
- 1 lemon, skinned

Directions:

1. Thoroughly wash the entire components under running cold water and run them through a juicer.

2. Put the juice into 2 glasses and serve with ice.

Per serving: Calories: 117kcal; Fat: 0g; Protein: 1g; Carbs: 30g

Kale With Healthy Apples Green Juice

Preparation time: 5 mins

Cooking time: 0 mins

Servings: 1

Ingredients:

- 2 cups of Swiss chard
- 1 cup of kale
- 2 carrots
- 2 celery stalks
- 2 apples

Directions:

1. Include the greens to a juicer and method along with apples, carrots, and celery stalks.

2. Pour the juice into a glass then drink immediately.

Per serving: Calories: 133kcal; Fat: 0g; Protein: 2g; Carbs: 33g

ENERGIZING JUICES

Orange, Cherry, Carrot, And Cucumber Juice

Preparation time: 10 minutes

Cooking time: 0 minutes

Servings: 2

Ingredients:

- 2 oranges, peeled and sectioned
- 2 cups fresh cherries, pitted
- 2 carrots, peeled and roughly chopped
- 1 cucumber, roughly chopped

Directions:

1. Add all ingredients into a juicer and extract the juice according to the manufacturer's method.

2. Pour into 2 glasses and serve immediately.

Per serving: Calories: 237kcal; Fat: 0.4g; Protein: 5.5g; Carbs: 58.1g

Apple, Beet, And Carrot Juice

Preparation time: 10 minutes

Cooking time: 0 minutes

Servings: 2

Ingredients:

- 2 large-sized carrots, peeled and chopped
- 2 medium-sized red beetroots, trimmed, peeled, and chopped
- 1 large-sized red apple, cored and quartered
- 1 large-sized green apple, cored and quartered

Directions:

1. Add all ingredients into a juicer and extract the juice according to the manufacturer's method.

2. Pour into 2 glasses and serve immediately.

Per serving: Calories: 284kcal; Fat: 0.9g; Protein: 4.3g; Carbs: 71.8g

Clementine, Fruit, And Veggie Juice

Preparation time: 10 minutes

Cooking time: 0 minutes

Servings: 2

Ingredients:

- 2 beetroots, peeled and roughly chopped
- 2 carrots, peeled and roughly chopped
- 2 green apples, cored and quartered
- 1 clementine, peeled
- 7–8 fresh strawberries, hulled
- 2 tbsp fresh lemon juice
- 2 cups of filtered water

Directions:

1. Add all ingredients into a juicer and extract the juice according to the manufacturer's method.

2. Pour into 2 glasses and serve immediately.

Per serving: Calories: 282kcal; Fat: 1.3g; Protein: 4.2g; Carbs: 67.3g

Apple, Pear, Orange, And Celery Juice

Preparation time: 10 minutes

Cooking time: 0 minutes

Servings: 2

Ingredients:

- 4 apples, cored and quartered
- 4 pears, cored and quartered
- 2 oranges, peeled, seeded, and sectioned
- 6 celery stalks

Directions:

1. Add all ingredients into a juicer and extract the juice according to the manufacturer's method.

2. Pour into 2 glasses and serve immediately.

Per serving: Calories: 568kcal; Fat: 1.7g; Protein: 4.8g; Carbs: 128.7g

Apple And Orange Juice

Preparation time: 10 minutes

Cooking time: 0 minutes

Servings: 2

Ingredients:

• 2 large-sized gala apples, cored and quartered

• 2 oranges, peeled and sectioned

• 1/2–3/4 cup filtered water

• 1 tsp honey

Directions:

1. Add all ingredients to a high-power blender and pulse until well combined.

2. Through a cheesecloth-lined sieve, strain the juice and pour it into 2 glasses.

3. Serve immediately.

Per serving: Calories: 224kcal; Fat: 0.6g; Protein: 2.4g; Carbs: 58.2g

Carrot, Beet, And Pomegranate Juice

Preparation time: 10 minutes

Cooking time: 0 minutes

Servings: 2

Ingredients:

• 4 carrots, peeled and roughly chopped

• 2 beetroots, peeled and roughly chopped

• 2 pomegranates, arils removed

Directions:

1. Add all ingredients into a juicer and extract the juice according to the manufacturer's method.

2. Pour into 2 glasses and serve immediately.

Per serving: Calories: 216kcal; Fat: 0.3g; Protein: 4.5g; Carbs: 52.9g

Apple, Carrot, Lemon & Ginger Juice

Preparation time: 10 minutes

Cooking time: 0 minutes

Servings: 2

Ingredients:

• 4 apples, cored and quartered

• 5 carrots, peeled and roughly chopped

• (1-inch) piece of fresh ginger, peeled

• 1/2 of lemon, peeled

Directions:

1. Add all ingredients into a juicer and extract the juice according to the manufacturer's method.

2. Pour into 2 glasses and serve immediately.

Per serving: Calories: 299kcal; Fat: 0.9g; Protein: 2.6g; Carbs: 77.6g

Kiwi, Apple, And Celery Juice

Preparation time: 10 minutes

Cooking time: 0 minutes

Servings: 2

Ingredients:

- 1 kiwi fruit, peeled
- 2 gala apples, cored and quartered
- 2 celery stalks

Directions:

1. Add all ingredients into a juicer and extract the juice according to the manufacturer's method.

2. Pour into 2 glasses and serve immediately.

Per serving: Calories: 307kcal; Fat: 1.5g; Protein: 2.7g; Carbs: 79.3g

Apple, Pear, Cumber, And Celery Juice

Preparation time: 10 minutes

Cooking time: 0 minutes

Servings: 2

Ingredients:

- 2 large-sized apples, cored and quartered
- 2 large-sized pears, cored and quartered
- 2 large-sized cucumbers, roughly chopped, sliced
- 2 celery stalks

Directions:

1. Add all ingredients into a juicer and extract the juice according to the manufacturer's method.

2. Pour into 2 glasses and serve immediately.

Per serving: Calories: 309kcal; Fat: 1.2g; Protein: 4.5g; Carbs: 79.8g

Cayenne Fruit And Veggie Juice

Preparation time: 10 minutes

Cooking time: 0 minutes

Servings: 2

Ingredients:

- 2 cups fresh kale
- 1 large-sized cucumber
- 2 celery stalks
- 2 red apples, cored and quartered
- 1/2 cup frozen white grapes
- 1/2 cup frozen watermelon
- 1 tbsp fresh lemon juice
- Pinch of cayenne pepper

Directions:

1. Add all ingredients except for cayenne pepper into a juicer and extract the juice according to the manufacturer's method.

2. Pour into 2 glasses and stir in cayenne pepper.

3. Serve immediately.

Per serving: Calories: 203kcal; Fat: 0.8g; Protein: 4.1g; Carbs: 50.8g

Apple, Kiwi, Spinach, And Celery Juice

Preparation time: 10 minutes

Cooking time: 0 minutes

Servings: 2

Ingredients:

- 1 cup coconut water with pulp
- 1 cup fresh spinach
- 2 celery stalks
- 1 kiwi fruit, peeled
- 1 Granny Smith apple, cored and quartered
- (1-inch) piece of fresh ginger

Directions:

1. Add all ingredients to a high-power blender and pulse until well combined.

2. Through a cheesecloth-lined sieve, strain the juice and pour it into 2 glasses.

3. Serve immediately.

Per serving: Calories: 141kcal; Fat: 1.1g; Protein: 2.8g; Carbs: 33.7g

Apple, Carrot, And Celery Juice

Preparation time: 10 minutes

Cooking time: 0 minutes

Servings: 2

Ingredients:

• 5 carrots, peeled and chopped

• 1 large-sized apple, cored and quartered

• 2 celery stalks

• (1/2-inch) piece of fresh ginger, peeled and chopped

• 1/2 of lemon

Directions:

1. Add all ingredients into a juicer and extract the juice according to the manufacturer's method.

2. Pour into 2 glasses and serve immediately.

Per serving: Calories: 126kcal; Fat: 0.3g; Protein: 1.8g; Carbs: 31.6g

Blueberry, Apple, Beet, And Cucumber Juice

Preparation time: 10 minutes

Cooking time: 0 minutes

Servings: 2

Ingredients:

• 1 cup fresh blueberries

• 2 apples, cored and quartered

• 1 cucumber, roughly chopped

• 1 beetroot, roughly chopped

• 1/4 of lemon, peeled

• 1/2 cup filtered water

Directions:

1. Add all ingredients to a high-power blender and pulse until well combined.

2. Through a cheesecloth-lined sieve, strain the juice and pour it into 2 glasses.

3. Serve immediately.

Per serving: Calories: 260kcal; Fat: 1.1g; Protein: 3.3g; Carbs: 67.1g

Apple, Celery, And Cucumber Juice

Preparation time: 10 minutes

Cooking time: 0 minutes

Servings: 2

Ingredients:

• 2 large-sized apples, cored and quartered

• 6 celery stalks

• 2 medium-sized cucumbers, roughly chopped

Directions:

1. Add all ingredients into a juicer and extract the juice according to the manufacturer's method.

2. Pour into 2 glasses and serve immediately.

Per serving: Calories: 170kcal; Fat: 0.9g; Protein: 3g; Carbs: 44.9g

Carrot And Parsley Juice

Preparation time: 10 minutes

Cooking time: 0 minutes

Servings: 2

Ingredients:

• 8 large-sized carrots, peeled and roughly chopped

• 1/4 cup fresh parsley

Directions:

1. Add all ingredients into a juicer and extract the juice according to the manufacturer's method.

2. Pour into 2 glasses and serve immediately.

Per serving: Calories: 103kcal; Fat: 0.1g; Protein: 2.2g; Carbs: 24.5g

Apple, Pear, Carrot, And Celery Juice

Preparation time: 10 minutes

Cooking time: 0 minutes

Servings: 2

Ingredients:

• 2 medium-sized apples, cored and quartered

• 2 medium-sized pears, cored and quartered

• 2 large-sized carrots, peeled and roughly chopped

• 2 celery stalks

Directions:

1. Add all ingredients into a juicer and extract the juice according to the manufacturer's method.

2. Pour into 2 glasses and serve immediately.

Per serving: Calories: 292kcal; Fat: 0.8g; Protein: 2.6g; Carbs: 75.6g

Gingered And Lemony Fruit And Veggie Juice

Preparation time: 10 minutes

Cooking time: 0 minutes

Servings: 2

Ingredients:

• 1 medium-sized pomegranate, arils removed

• 1 medium-sized apple, cored and quartered

• 1/4 cup beetroot, peeled and roughly chopped

• 1 large-sized tomato

• 1 medium-sized carrot, peeled and roughly chopped

• (1-inch) piece fresh ginger, peeled

• 1 lemon, seeded

Directions:

1. Add all ingredients into a juicer and extract the juice according to the manufacturer's method.

2. Pour into 2 glasses and serve immediately.

Per serving: Calories: 158kcal; Fat: 0.6g; Protein: 2.5g; Carbs: 39.7g

Pear, Celery, And Greens Juice

Preparation time: 10 minutes

Cooking time: 0 minutes

Servings: 2

Ingredients:

• 2 pears, cored and quartered

• 2 cups fresh spinach

• 2 cups fresh kale

• 2 celery stalks

Directions:

1. Add all ingredients into a juicer and extract the juice according to the manufacturer's method.

2. Pour into 2 glasses and serve immediately.

Per serving: Calories: 224kcal; Fat: 0.6g; Protein: 4.1g; Carbs: 56.3g

Watermelon, Apple, And Tomato Juice

Preparation time: 10 minutes

Cooking time: 0 minutes

Servings: 2

Ingredients:

• 2 1/2 cups seedless watermelon, cubed

• 1 cup apples, cored and quartered

• 1 cup tomatoes, chopped

Directions:

1. Add all ingredients into a juicer and extract the juice according to the manufacturer's method.

2. Pour into 2 glasses and serve immediately.

Per serving: Calories: 131kcal; Fat: 0.6g; Protein: 2.2g; Carbs: 33.2g

Kiwi, Apple, And Grapes Juice

Preparation time: 10 minutes

Cooking time: 0 minutes

Servings: 2

Ingredients:

• 2 large-sized kiwis, peeled and chopped

• 2 large-sized green apples, cored and quartered

• 2 cups seedless green grapes

• 1 tsp fresh lime juice

Directions:

1. Add all ingredients into a juicer and extract the juice according to the manufacturer's method.

2. Pour into 2 glasses and serve immediately.

Per serving: Calories: 304kcal; Fat: 2.2g; Protein: 6.2g; Carbs: 79g

ANTI-OXIDANT JUICES

Chard With Juicy Pear Boost

Preparation time: 5 minutes

Cooking time: 0 minutes

Servings: 2

Ingredients:

- 4 small celery stalks
- 4 small Swiss chard leaves
- 1 firm pear
- 1/2 lemon
- 1/2 large cucumber

Directions:

1. Peel, cut, deseed, and/or chop the ingredients as needed.

2. Place a container under the juicer's spout.

3. Feed the ingredients one at a time, in the order listed, through the juicer.

4. Stir the juice and pour it into glasses to serve.

Per serving: Calories: 60kcal; Fat: 1g; Protein: 3g; Carbs: 14g

Watermelon, Orange, And Mint Juice

Preparation time: 10 minutes

Cooking time: 0 minutes

Servings: 2

Ingredients:

- 1 cup fresh orange juice.
- 4 cups seedless watermelon, chopped
- 5–6 fresh mint leaves
- 1–2 tbsp honey

Directions:

1. Add all ingredients to a high-power blender and pulse for about 15 to 20 seconds.

2. Through a cheesecloth-lined sieve, strain the juice and pour it into 2 glasses.

3. Serve immediately.

Per serving: Calories: 182kcal; Fat: 0.7g; Protein: 2.9g; Carbs: 44.9g

Sprout With Aloe Cleanser

Preparation time: 10 minutes

Cooking time: 0 minutes

Servings: 1

Ingredients:

- 1/4 cup alfalfa sprouts
- 1 pear
- 1 cup cabbage
- 1/4 cup aloe vera juice

Directions:

1. Wash the alfalfa sprouts, pear, and cabbage.

2. Cut the pear into quarters, removing the core and seeds, but leaving the peel intact.

3. Cut the cabbage in half, then slice or chop it into smaller pieces.

4. Place a pitcher under the juicer's spout to collect the juice.

5. Feed the first 3 ingredients through the juicer's intake tube in the order listed.

6. When the juice stops flowing, remove the pitcher, add the aloe vera juice, and stir.

7. Serve immediately.

Per serving: Calories: 91kcal; Fat: 0g; Protein: 3g; Carbs: 29g

Citrus Apple And Carrot Juice

Preparation time: 10 minutes

Cooking time: 0 minutes

Servings: 2

Ingredients:

- 2 large-sized apples, cored and quartered
- 4 medium-sized carrots, peeled and chopped
- 2 medium-size grapefruits, peeled and seeded
- 2 tsp fresh lemon juice

Directions:

1. Add all ingredients into a juicer and extract the juice according to the manufacturer's method.

2. Pour into 2 glasses and serve immediately.

Per serving: Calories: 208kcal; Fat: 0.6g; Protein: 2.4g; Carbs: 53.2g

Lemony Bell Pepper Boost

Preparation time: 5 minutes

Cooking time: 0 minutes

Servings: 3

Ingredients:

- 2 large yellow bell peppers
- 1 large celery stalk
- 1 lemon
- 1-inch piece of fresh ginger root
- 1 pink or red grapefruit, peeled

Directions:

1. Peel, cut, deseed, and/or chop the ingredients as needed.

2. Place a container under the juicer's spout.

3. Feed the ingredients one at a time, in the order listed, through the juicer.

4. Stir the juice and pour it into glasses to serve.

Per serving: Calories: 44kcal; Fat: 0g; Protein: 1g; Carbs: 11g

Body Dew Juice

Preparation time: 10 minutes

Cooking time: 0 minutes

Servings: 1

Ingredients:

- 1 cup of blackberry
- 1 kiwi
- 1 medium-size pear
- Peppermint as optional
- 1/4 of peeled and cored pineapple

Directions:

1. Peel and core the pineapple.

2. Juice everything.

3. Stir or shake extracted juice.

4. Serve.

Per serving: Calories: 209kcal; Fat: 1.2g; Protein: 5g; Carbs: 56g

Spinach With Pear-Grapefruit Cooler

Preparation time: 5 minutes

Cooking time: 0 minutes

Servings: 1

Ingredients:

- 4 medium celery stalks
- 1/2 large cucumber
- Handful spinach

- 1 firm pear
- 1/2 pink or red grapefruit, peeled
- 1 cup pineapple

Directions:

1. Peel, cut, deseed, and/or chop the ingredients as needed.

2. Place a container under the juicer's spout.

3. Feed the ingredients one at a time, in the order listed, through the juicer.

4. Stir the juice and pour it into glasses to serve.

Per serving: Calories: 335kcal; Fat: 0g; Protein: 12g; Carbs: 78g

Orange, Grapefruit, And Apple Juice

Preparation time: 10 minutes

Cooking time: 0 minutes

Servings: 2

Ingredients:

- 3 large-sized apples, cored and quartered
- 2 large-sized oranges, peeled and sectioned
- 2 large-sized of grapefruits, peeled and sectioned
- 1/2 of lemon, peeled
- (1/2-inch) piece of fresh ginger, peeled

Directions:

1. Add all ingredients into a juicer and extract the juice according to the manufacturer's method.

2. Pour into 2 glasses and serve immediately.

Per serving: Calories: 306kcal; Fat: 1g; Protein: 3.6g; Carbs: 79.1g

Asparagus And Kale Salad

Preparation time: 5 minutes

Cooking time: 0 minutes

Servings: 2

Ingredients:

- 8 asparagus spears
- 1/2 lemon
- 4 medium kale leaves
- 4 small carrots
- 8 small celery stalks
- 1 large cucumber

Directions:

1. Peel, cut, deseed, and/or chop the ingredients as needed.

2. Place a container under the juicer's spout.

3. Feed the ingredients one at a time, in the order listed, through the juicer.

4. Stir the juice and pour it into glasses to serve.

Per serving: Calories: 90kcal; Fat: 1g; Protein: 4g; Carbs: 19g

Broccoli With Carrot Immunity Plus

Preparation time: 15 minutes

Cooking time: 0 minutes

Servings: 1

Ingredients:

- 1 small beet
- 2 carrots
- 8 celery ribs
- 1 broccoli stalk

• 2 garlic cloves, peeled

Directions:

1. Wash all the ingredients except the garlic.

2. Remove any greens from the beet and save them for juicing later. Cut the beet into quarters.

3. Trim the ends from the carrots and celery, then cut them into 4-inch pieces.

4. Remove the stalk from the broccoli crown with a knife and discard or save to juice later. Cut the crown into small florets.

5. Place a pitcher under the juicer's spout to collect the juice.

6. Feed each ingredient through the juicer's intake tube in the order listed.

7. When the juice stops flowing, remove the pitcher and stir the juice.

8. Serve immediately.

Per serving: Calories: 120kcal; Fat: 1g; Protein: 7g; Carbs: 34g

Lime With Gingery Sensation

Preparation time: 10 minutes

Cooking time: 0 minutes

Servings: 1

Ingredients:

• 3 medium apples

• 2 big sticks of celery

• 1 cucumber

• 1 ginger root thumb

• 1 lime

Directions:

1. Peel the lime as optional.

2. Process everything through a juicer.

3. Shake achieved juice.

4. Drink.

Per serving: Calories: 221kcal; Fat: 1g; Protein: 4g; Carbs: 70g

Limey Tropical Fiesta

Preparation time: 10 minutes

Cooking time: 0 minutes

Servings: 1

Ingredients:

• 2 apples

• 4 kale leaves

• 1/2 of a peeled lime

• 1/2 a cup of cold coconut water

Directions:

1. Wash all fruits.

2. Peel the lime.

3. Juice kale, lime, and apples with a juicer.

4. Pour extracted juice into a glass with cold coconut water.

5. Serve.

Per serving: Calories: 174kcal; Fat: 1g; Protein: 3g; Carbs: 73g

Berries And Apple Juice

Preparation time: 10 minutes

Cooking time: 0 minutes

Servings: 2

Ingredients:

• 1 Cup fresh blackberries

• 1 Cup fresh blueberries

• 1 Cup fresh raspberries

- 2 Large-sized apples, cored and quartered

Directions:

1. Add all ingredients into a juicer and extract the juice according to the manufacturer's method.

2. Pour into 2 glasses and serve immediately.

Per serving: Calories: 220kcal; Fat: 1.4g; Protein: 2.9g; Carbs: 85.2g

Lemony Papaya And Kale Mix

Preparation time: 15 minutes

Cooking time: 0 minutes

Servings: 1

Ingredients:

- 1 cup papaya
- 6 kale leaves
- 1 fresh turmeric root
- 1 lemon

Directions:

1. Wash the kale, turmeric root, and lemon.

2. Cut the papaya in half lengthwise. Scoop out seeds and discard, then scoop out the flesh and discard the papaya skin.

3. Slice off a 2-inch piece of the turmeric root.

4. Peel the lemon and cut it into quarters.

5. Place a pitcher under the juicer's spout to collect the juice.

6. Feed each ingredient through the juicer's intake tube in the order listed.

7. When the juice stops flowing, remove the pitcher, and stir the juice.

8. Serve immediately.

Per serving: Calories: 127kcal; Fat: 0g; Protein: 8g; Carbs: 36g

Blood Orange Booster

Preparation time: 10 minutes

Cooking time: 0 minutes

Servings: 1

Ingredients:

- 2 blood oranges, peeled
- 1/4 of pineapple
- 1 big banana
- A couple of ice

Directions:

1. Peel the oranges, leave the white pith.

2. Juice the oranges and pineapple.

3. Pour the juice with peeled banana and ice into the blender.

4. Blend.

5. This drink can provide a quick energy boost, making you more alert, and also helps to regulate blood sugar levels.

Per serving: Calories: 224kcal; Fat: 0g; Protein: 0g; Carbs: 29g

Cucumber Chard Immune Support

Preparation time: 5 minutes

Cooking time: 0 minutes

Servings: 2

Ingredients:

- 8 small celery stalks
- 4 cups Swiss chard
- 2 oranges, peeled
- 1/2 large cucumber

Directions:

1. Peel, cut, deseed, and/or chop the ingredients as needed.

2. Place a container under the juicer's spout.

3. Feed the ingredients one at a time, in the order listed, through the juicer.

4. Stir the juice and pour it into glasses to serve.

Per serving: Calories: 133kcal; Fat: 1g; Protein: 4g; Carbs: 31g

Strawberry And Orange Juice

Preparation time: 10 minutes

Cooking time: 0 minutes

Servings: 2

Ingredients:

- 1 Cup fresh strawberries, hulled
- 2 Cups chilled fresh orange juice
- 1 Tbsp. maple syrup

Directions:

1. Add all ingredients to a high-power blender and pulse for about 15 to 20 seconds.

2. Through a cheesecloth-lined sieve, strain the juice and pour it into 4 glasses.

3. Serve immediately.

Per serving: Calories: 161kcal; Fat: 0.7g; Protein: 2.2g; Carbs: 38g

Spinach With Cherry Ginger Blast

Preparation time: 15 minutes

Cooking time: 0 minutes

Servings: 1

Ingredients:

- 1 1/2 cups spinach

- 1 cup cherries
- 1 fresh ginger root
- 1 cup sparkling water

Directions:

1. Wash the spinach, cherries, and ginger root.

2. Remove the cherry pits and stems.

3. Slice off a 2-inch piece of ginger root.

4. Place a pitcher under the juicer's spout to collect the juice.

5. Feed each ingredient through the juicer's intake tube in the order listed.

6. When the juice stops flowing, remove the pitcher and stir the juice.

7. Serve immediately.

Per serving: Calories: 76kcal; Fat: 0g; Protein: 2g; Carbs: 21g

Lemony Apple, Cucumber, And Celery Juice

Preparation time: 10 minutes

Cooking time: 0 minutes

Servings: 2

Ingredients:

- 3 large-sized apples, cored and quartered
- 2 large-sized cucumbers, roughly chopped
- 4 celery stalks
- (1-inch) piece of fresh ginger, peeled
- 1 lemon, peeled

Directions:

1. Add all ingredients into a juicer and extract the juice according to the manufacturer's method.

2. Pour into 2 glasses and serve immediately.

Per serving: Calories: 230kcal; Fat: 1.1g; Protein: 3.3g; Carbs: 59.5g

Grapy Romaine Immune Booster

Preparation time: 10 mins

Cooking time: 0 mins

Servings: 2

Ingredients:

- 2 large celery stalks
- 2 large romaine leaves
- 1 pink or red grapefruit, peeled

Directions:

1. To prepare the items, you may be required to skin, slice, de-seed, or mince them.

2. Put a bowl at the spot where the juice will come out of the juicer.

3. Move the components thru the juicer one by one, following the sequence in which they are written.

4. After giving this a mix, put the juice into the glasses to serve.

Per serving: Calories: 71kcal; Fat: 1g; Protein: 5g; Carbs: 14g

DETOXIFYING AND CLEANSING JUICES

Potato Kale Detox

Preparation time: 10 mins

Cooking time: 0 mins

Servings: 3

Ingredients:

- 4 extra-large carrots
- 2 large kale leaves
- 1 small, sweet potato, peeled

Directions:

1. To prepare the items, you may be required to skin, slice, de-seed, or mince them.

2. Put a bowl at the spot where the juice will come out of the juicer.

3. Move the components thru the juicer one by one, following the sequence in which they are written.

4. Alternate ingredients, finishing with the sweet potato.

5. After giving this a mix, put the juice into the glasses to serve.

Per iserving: i Calories: i27kcal; iFat: i1g; iProtein: i1g; iCarbs: i9g i

Artichoke With Apple Beauty Juice

Preparation time: 20 mins

Cooking time: 0 mins

Servings: 1

Ingredients:

- 1 artichoke
- 1 green apple
- 1 cup spinach
- 1 celery rib

Directions:

1. Wash all the ingredients.

2. Prepare the artichoke per the instructions in the preparation tip.

3. Remove the apple core and discard. Cut the apple into quarters, leaving the peel intact.

4. Cut the sides from the celery, then slice into 4-inch pieces.

5. Put a pitcher beneath the juicer's spout to collect the juice. Then, feed each ingredient through the juicer's intake tube in the order listed.

6. When the juice stops flowing, remove the pitcher and stir the juice.

7. Serve instantly.

Per serving: Calories: 75kcal; Fat: 0g; Protein: 4g; Carbs: 25g

Garlicky Radish Detox Juice

Preparation time: 5 mins

Cooking time: 0 mins

Servings: 1

Ingredients:

- 2 garlic cloves
- 3 medium carrots
- 1 medium beet
- 1 radish
- A handful of parsley

Directions:

1. Peel the beet, carrots, radish, and garlic and wash the parsley.

2. Run all ingredients through a juicer and drink immediately.

3. Great to drink 1–2 times a day.

Per serving: Calories: 90kcal; Fat: 0g; Protein: 2g; Carbs: 21g

Cabbage And Cucumber Body Cleanse

Preparation time: 5 mins

Cooking time: 0 mins

Servings: 1

Ingredients:

• 1/2 medium cucumber

• 1 smallish beet

• A handful of red or green cabbage leaves

• 2 medium carrots

Directions:

1. Thoroughly wash the vegetables.

2. Cut the carrot ends and discard the greens.

3. Peel the beet and quarter it.

4. Pass the entire components through a juicer, put them into a glass, and drink immediately.

Per serving: Calories: 56kcal; Fat: 0g; Protein: 1g; Carbs: 13g

Parsley With Cabbage Detox

Preparation time: 10 mins

Cooking time: 0 mins

Servings: 2

Ingredients:

• 1 Cup red cabbage

• 2 Cups black, purple, or red grapes

• 12 parsley sprigs

• 2 Large celery stalks

Directions:

1. To prepare the items, you may be required to skin, slice, de-seed, or mince them.

2. Put a bowl at the spot where the juice will come out of the juicer.

3. Move the components thru the juicer one by one, following the sequence in which they are written.

4. Alternate ingredients, finishing with the sweet potato.

5. After giving this a mix, put the juice into the glasses to serve.

Per serving: Calories: 133kcal; Fat: 0g; Protein: 2g; Carbs: 32g

Zucchini With Bok Choy Blend

Preparation time: 10 mins

Cooking time: 0 mins

Servings: 2

Ingredients:

• 1 medium zucchini

• 2 cups black, purple, or red grapes

• 4 small Bok choy stems

Directions:

1. To prepare the items, you may be required to skin, slice, de-seed, or mince them.

2. Put a bowl at the spot where the juice will come out of the juicer.

3. Move the components thru the juicer one by one, following the sequence in which they are written.

4. Alternate ingredients, finishing with the sweet potato.

5. After giving this a mix, put the juice into the glasses to serve.

Per serving: Calories: 105kcal; Fat: 0g; Protein: 1g; Carbs: 23g

Pineapple, Banana, And Kale Juice

Preparation time: 10 mins

Cooking time: 0 mins

Servings: 2

Ingredients:

- 3 cups pineapple chunks
- 1 ripe banana, skinned
- 3 cups fresh kale leaves

Directions:

1. Add all ingredients into a juicer and excerpt the juice according to the producer's method.

2. Put into 2 glasses and serve instantly.

Per serving: Calories: 225kcal; Fat: 0.5g; Protein: 5g; Carbs: 56.5g

Kale With Chard And Celery Cleanse

Preparation time: 15 mins

Cooking time: 0 mins

Servings: 2

Ingredients:

- 2 large celery stalks
- 1 large kale leaf
- 2 cups spinach
- 1 large Swiss chard leaf
- 2 green apples
- 8 parsley or cilantro sprigs
- 1 large cucumber

Directions:

1. To prepare the items, you may be required to skin, slice, de-seed, or mince them.

2. Put a bowl at the spot where the juice will come out of the juicer.

3. Move the components thru the juicer one by one, following the sequence in which they are written.

4. Alternate ingredients, finishing with the sweet potato.

5. After giving this a mix, put the juice into the glasses to serve.

Per serving: Calories: 127kcal; Fat: 0g; Protein: 3g; Carbs: 31g

Turmeric With Ginger Green Juice

Preparation time: 5 mins

Cooking time: 0 mins

Servings: 1

Ingredients:

- 6 carrots
- 1 romaine heart
- 1 celery ribs
- 1 orange
- 1 fresh ginger root
- 1 fresh turmeric root

Directions:

1. Wash the entire components.

2. Trim the ends from the carrots, romaine, and celery, afterwards slice these into 4-inch pieces.

3. Skin the orange and cut it into quarters.

4. Slice off 1/2-inch pieces of the ginger root and the turmeric root.

5. Put a pitcher beneath the juicer's spout to collect the juice.

6. Feed each ingredient through the juicer's intake tube in the order listed.

7. When the juice stops flowing, remove the pitcher and stir the juice.

8. Serve instantly.

Per serving: Calories: 151kcal; Fat: 2g; Protein: 7g; Carbs: 46g

Whole Juicy Detox Drink

Preparation time: 10 mins

Cooking time: 0 mins

Servings: 1

Ingredients:

• 3 ribs of celery (organic if possible)

• Big handful of spinach (organic if possible or organic baby spinach)

• 2 stalks of asparagus (organic if possible)

• 1 large tomato (organic if possible)

• 1 carrot (organic if possible)

Directions:

1. Peel the tomato, carrot, and asparagus.

2. Next cut and chop the veggies.

3. Put all the fruits and veggies from the ingredients list into your favorite juicer or blender or a combination of juicer/blender (Nutribullet) and strictly follow the directions of the manual that comes with your machine.

4. Your blender manual will tell you what buttons to push and what speed to use.

5. Juice the softer textures first.

6. You will see that when you are juicing the crunchier veggies, they will help you push the softer and more delicate ones through the blades.

7. Juice and blend all the ingredients from the list above together as per instructions.

8. Enjoy!

Per serving: Calories: 54kcal; Fat: 0.5g; Protein: 2.5g; Carbs: 12g

Watermelon And Rosemary Juice

Preparation time: 10 mins

Cooking time: 0 mins

Servings: 4

Ingredients:

• 26 oz fresh iwatermelon, cubed

• 1 tbsp fresh rosemary

• 2 tbsps. fresh lime juice

• 2 tbsps. isugar

Directions:

1. Include the entire components to a high-power blender and beat till well combined.

2. Through a cheesecloth-lined sieve, strain the juice and pour it into 2 glasses.

3. Serve immediately.

Per serving: Calories: 81kcal; Fat: 0.4g; Protein: 1.1g; Carbs: 20.5g

Turmeric With Potato And Orange Roots

Preparation time: 10 mins

Cooking time: 0 mins

Servings: 2

Ingredients:

- 4 large carrots
- 1-inch piece of fresh turmeric root
- 1 small, sweet potato, peeled
- Freshly ground black pepper (optional)

Directions:

1. To prepare the items, you may be required to skin, slice, de-seed, or mince them.

2. Put a bowl at the spot where the juice will come out of the juicer.

3. Move the components thru the juicer one by one, following the sequence in which they are written.

4. Alternate the produce, finishing with the sweet potato.

5. Stir the black pepper (if used) directly into the juice to increase your absorption of the curcumin in the turmeric.

Per serving: Calories: 86kcal; Fat: 0g; Protein: 2g; Carbs: 20g

Plum With Kale Cocktail

Preparation time: 10 mins

Cooking time: 0 mins

Servings: 2

Ingredients:

- 1 cup red cabbage
- 1 medium kale leaves
- 1 medium red apple
- 1/2 red or black plum
- 1/2 large cucumber

Directions:

1. To prepare the items, you may be required to skin, slice, de-seed, or mince them.

2. Put a bowl at the spot where the juice will come out of the juicer.

3. Move the components thru the juicer one by one, following the sequence in which they are written.

4. Alternate ingredients, finishing with the sweet potato.

5. After giving this a mix, put the juice into the glasses to serve.

Per serving: Calories: 80kcal; Fat: 0g; Protein: 1g; Carbs: 20g

Arugula Detox Juice With Celery

Preparation time: 5 mins

Cooking time: 0 mins

Servings: 1

Ingredients:

- Handful arugula
- 1-inch piece of fresh ginger root
- 1 large celery stalk
- 1 medium green apple

Directions:

1. To prepare the items, you may be required to skin, slice, de-seed, or mince them.

2. Put a bowl at the spot where the juice will come out of the juicer.

3. Move the components thru the juicer one by one, following the sequence in which they are written.

4. Alternate ingredients, finishing with the sweet potato.

5. After giving this a mix, put the juice into the glasses to serve.

Per serving: Calories: 138kcal; Fat: 2g; Protein: 10g; Carbs: 41g

Berries And Carrot Juice

Preparation time: 10 mins

Cooking time: 0 mins

Servings: 2

Ingredients:

- 1 1/2 cups fresh blueberries
- 1 1/2 cups fresh strawberries, hulled
- 1 cup fresh raspberries
- 4 medium-sized carrots, peeled and roughly chopped

Directions:

1. Add all ingredients into a juicer and excerpt the juice according to the producer's method.

2. Put in 2 glasses and serve instantly.

Per serving: Calories: 89kcal; Fat: 0.6g; Protein: 1.6g; Carbs: 21.7g

Lemony Red Velvet

Preparation time: 10 mins

Cooking time: 0 mins

Servings: 1

Ingredients:

- 2 medium apples
- 4 medium carrots
- 1/4 head of small red cabbage
- 1/2 thumb ginger root ginger root
- 4 handfuls of spinach

- 1/2 of fruit lemon (Recommended peeled for less-bitter taste)

Directions:

1. Wash the fruits and vegetables thoroughly

2. Put them through the juicer and enjoy

Per serving: Calories: 208kcal; Fat: 1.4g; Protein: 6g; Carbs: 66g

Watermelon With Pineapple Cleansing Mix

Preparation time: 10 mins

Cooking time: 0 mins

Servings: 2

Ingredients:

- 2 large kale leaves
- 1 cup pineapple
- 2 cups watermelon

Directions:

1. To prepare the items, you may be required to skin, slice, de-seed, or mince them.

2. Put a bowl at the spot where the juice will come out of the juicer.

3. Move the components thru the juicer one by one, following the sequence in which they are written.

4. Alternate ingredients, finishing with the sweet potato.

5. After giving this a mix, put the juice into the glasses to serve.

Per serving: Calories: 121kcal; Fat: 0g; Protein: 1g; Carbs: 31g

Lemony Spinach Veggie Cleanser

Preparation time: 15 mins

Cooking time: 0 mins

Servings: 2

Ingredients:

- 3 cups spinach
- 1/2 small, sweet potato, peeled
- 8 parsley sprigs
- 1/2 medium lemon
- 4 large celery stalks

Directions:

1. To prepare the items, you may be required to skin, slice, de-seed, or mince them.

2. Put a bowl at the spot where the juice will come out of the juicer.

3. Move the components thru the juicer one by one, following the sequence in which they are written.

4. Alternate ingredients, finishing with the sweet potato.

5. After giving this a mix, put the juice into the glasses to serve.

Per serving: Calories: 20kcal; Fat: 0g; Protein: 2g; Carbs: 4g

Carroty Radish Cleanser

Preparation time: 10 mins

Cooking time: 0 mins

Servings: 1

Ingredients:

- 1 apple (organic if possible)
- 5 carrots (organic if possible)
- 1 beet (organic if possible)
- 1 cucumber (organic if possible)
- 1 black radish (organic if possible)

Directions:

1. Peel the apple, the radish, the beets (or buy them already prepared and ready to use), carrots, and cucumber.

2. Next cut and chop the veggies.

3. Put all the veggies from the ingredients list into your favorite juicer or blender or a combination of juicer/blender and strictly follow the directions of the manual that comes with your machine.

4. The manual will tell you what buttons to push and what speed to use.

5. Juice the softer textures first. You will see that when you are juicing the crunchier fruits and veggies first, they will help you push the softer and more delicate ones through the blades.

6. Juice and blend all the ingredients from the list above together as per instructions.

7. Enjoy this refreshing and hydrating Beet and Black Radish Liver Cleanser!

Per serving: Calories: 316kcal; Fat: 2g; Protein: 8g; Carbs: 77g

Melony Tomato Cleanse

Preparation time: 10 mins

Cooking time: 0 mins

Servings: 1

Ingredients:

- 1 large tomato

- 1 large wedge melony
- Lemon 1/2 of fruit (Recommended peeled for less-bitter taste)

Directions:

1. Wash the fruits and vegetables thoroughly.

2. Put them through the juicer and relish.

Per serving: Calories: 135kcal; Fat: 1g; Protein: 4g; Carbs: 37g

Conversion Chart

Volume Equivalents (Liquid)

US Standard	US Standard (ounces)	Metric (approximate)
2 tablespoons	1 fl. oz.	30 mL
¼ cup	2 fl. oz.	60 mL
½ cup	4 fl. oz.	120 mL
1 cup	8 fl. oz.	240 mL
1½ cups	12 fl. oz.	355 mL
2 cups or 1 pint	16 fl. oz.	475 mL
4 cups or 1 quart	32 fl. oz.	1 L
1 gallon	128 fl. oz.	4 L

Volume Equivalents (Dry)

US Standard	Metric (approximate)
⅛ teaspoon	0.5 mL
¼ teaspoon	1 mL
½ teaspoon	2 mL
¾ teaspoon	4 mL
1 teaspoon	5 mL
1 tablespoon	15 mL
¼ cup	59 mL
⅓ cup	79 mL
½ cup	118 mL
⅔ cup	156 mL
¾ cup	177 mL
1 cup	235 mL
2 cups or 1 pint	475 mL
3 cups	700 mL
4 cups or 1 quart	1 L

Oven Temperatures

Fahrenheit (F)	Celsius (C) (approximate)
250°F	120°C
300°F	150°C
325°F	165°C
350°F	180°C
375°F	190°C
400°F	200°C
425°F	220°C
450°F	230°C

Weight Equivalents

US Standard	Metric (approximate)
1 tablespoon	15 g
½ ounce	15 g
1 ounce	30 g
2 ounces	60 g
4 ounces	115 g
8 ounces	225 g
12 ounces	340 g
16 ounces or 1 pound	455 g

30-Day Meal Plan

Days	Breakfast	Lunch	Dinner	Dessert
1	Spinach With Basil Refreshing Juice	Grapefruit Juice With Lemon And Orange	Watermelon, Orange, And Mint Juice	Turmeric With Ginger Green Juice
2	Juicy Spinach With Apple Lemonade	Arugula Watermelon Juice	Lemony Bell Pepper Boost	Parsley With Cabbage Detox
3	Melony Morning Booster	Apple, Beet, And Carrot Juice	Berry With Sparkling Pomegranate Juice	Lemony Spinach Veggie Cleanser
4	Fresh Morning Juice	Body Dew Juice	Parsley With Lettuce Special	Arugula Detox Juice With Celery
5	Kale With Parsley Morning Drink	Blueberry And Pineapple Juice	Kiwi, Apple, And Celery Juice	Melony Tomato Cleanse
6	Gingered Chard Red Juice	Gingered Carrot With Oregano Green Juice	Asparagus And Kale Salad	Lemony Red Velvet
7	Early-Berry Juice	Apple, Kiwi, Spinach, And Celery Juice	Watermelon, Plum, And Cherry Juice	Berries And Carrot Juice
8	Peach And Apple Morning Delight	Berries And Apple Juice	Pear, Spinach, Celery, And Parsley Juice	Turmeric With Potato And Orange Roots
9	Pineapple And Orange Juice	Berry With Cilantro And Banana Juice	Apple, Celery, And Cucumber Juice	Pineapple, Banana, And Kale Juice
10	Juicy Morning Blaster	Watermelon With Kale Green Juice	Cucumber Chard Immune Support	Artichoke With Apple Beauty Juice

11	Morning Cucumber And Berry Chard	Gingered And Lemony Fruit And Veggie Juice	Grape Nectar Juice	Garlicky Radish Detox Juice
12	Passionfruit Juice	Lemony Apple, Cucumber, And Celery Juice	Cucumber Grape Juice	Kale With Chard And Celery Cleanse
13	Apple And Lime Juice	Cilantro Kiwi Juice Blend	Watermelon, Apple, And Tomato Juice	Potato Kale Detox
14	Watermelon, Lime, And Ginger Juice	Lemony Kale And Celery Green Juice	Lime With Gingery Sensation	Cabbage And Cucumber Body Cleanse
15	Juicy Morning Glow	Blueberry, Apple, Beet, And Cucumber Juice	Banana Blackberry Fruit Juice	Zucchini With Bok Choy Blend
16	Limey Morning Blast	Spinach With Pear-Grapefruit Cooler	Purple Haze Juice	Watermelon And Rosemary Juice
17	Fresh Sunrise Drink	Sugared Avocado With Lemon Water	Apple, Pear, Orange, And Celery Juice	Whole Juicy Detox Drink
18	Strawberry And Parsley Juice	Kale With Healthy Apples Green Juice	Lemony Papaya And Kale Mix	Watermelon With Pineapple Cleansing Mix
19	Kale With Beet Red Juice	Carrot, Beet, And Pomegranate Juice	Beet With Berry And Apple Juice	Plum With Kale Cocktail
20	Green Citrus Drink	Broccoli With Carrot Immunity Plus	Tomato Beet Multi Juice	Carroty Radish Cleanser
21	Fresh Morning Juice	Juicy Tropical Island	Apple, Pear, Cumber, And Celery Juice	Parsley With Cabbage Detox

22	Early-Berry Juice	Horseradish Beet Juice	Spinach With Cherry Ginger Blast	Pineapple, Banana, And Kale Juice
23	Pineapple And Orange Juice	Apple, Pear, Carrot, And Celery Juice	Orange Basil Juice	Turmeric With Ginger Green Juice
24	Spinach With Basil Refreshing Juice	Orange, Grapefruit, And Apple Juice	Broccoli With Mellow Celery	Turmeric With Potato And Orange Roots
25	Juicy Morning Blaster	Orange, Carrot, And Lemon Juice	Apple And Orange Juice	Arugula Detox Juice With Celery
26	Melony Morning Booster	Citrus Apple, Spinach, And Celery Juice	Citrus Apple And Carrot Juice	Berries And Carrot Juice
27	Peach And Apple Morning Delight	Apple, Carrot, And Celery Juice	Apple And Grapes Juice	Melony Tomato Cleanse
28	Morning Cucumber And Berry Chard	Chard With Juicy Pear Boost	Spinach Vegetable Juice	Lemony Spinach Veggie Cleanser
29	Juicy Spinach With Apple Lemonade	Grapy Berry With Apple Juice	Pear, Celery, And Greens Juice	Artichoke With Apple Beauty Juice
30	Kale With Parsley Morning Drink	Cucumber Carrot Juice	Sprout With Aloe Cleanser	Lemony Red Velvet

Index

Pineapple And Orange Juice; 26
Pineapple, Banana, And Kale Juice; 62
Plum Juice; 29
Plum With Kale Cocktail; 64
Pomegranate Juice; 28
Potato Kale Detox; 60
Purple Haze Juice; 41
Radish Beet Juice; 42
Spinach Vegetable Juice; 38
Spinach With Basil Refreshing Juice; 21
Spinach With Cherry Ginger Blast; 57
Spinach With Pear-Grapefruit Cooler; 53
Sprout With Aloe Cleanser; 52
Strawberry And Orange Juice; 57

Strawberry And Parsley Juice; 24
Sugared Avocado With Lemon Water; 30
Tomato Beet Multi Juice; 39
Turmeric With Ginger Green Juice; 62
Turmeric With Potato And Orange Roots; 63
Watermelon And Rosemary Juice; 63
Watermelon With Kale Green Juice; 40
Watermelon With Pineapple Cleansing Mix; 65
Watermelon, Apple, And Tomato Juice; 50
Watermelon, Lime, And Ginger Juice; 21
Watermelon, Orange, And Mint Juice; 52
Watermelon, Plum, And Cherry Juice; 32
Whole Juicy Detox Drink; 63
Zucchini With Bok Choy Blend; 61

Conclusion

Juicing can be a great way to start a journey towards a healthier lifestyle for you as a beginner. It can be a fun experience, introducing you to the world of nutrition and inspiring you to take control of your health. Juicing helps you to get an abundance of essential vitamins, minerals and antioxidants into your diet, while removing toxins and providing your body with nourishment. In addition, juicing is a convenient way to get your daily dose of fruits and vegetables. As a beginner, it is important to take your time and start slow. Start with familiar fruits and vegetables that you know you like. Experiment with different combinations and find something that you enjoy. It is also important to remember to drink plenty of water and to stay hydrated. With a bit of practice, juicing can easily become a part of your everyday routine and help you to reach your health goals.

DOWNLOAD YOUR BONUS NOW !

HEART HEALTHY COOKBOOK

E-BOOK

EASY AND TASTY LOW-FAT RECIPES TO KEEP CHOLESTEROL AND BLOOD PRESSURE LEVELS DOWN

The "Heart Healthy Cookbook" is **100% FREE;** all you need to get is a name and email address. **It's super simple !**

TO DOWNLOAD THE BONUS SCAN THE QR CODE BELOW OR GO TO

https://l.linklyhq.com/l/1g3wX

Made in United States
Troutdale, OR
11/19/2023

14741079R00044